BRITISH FASHION DESIGNERS

HYWEL DAVIES

LAURENCE KING PUBLISHING

Published in 2009 by
Laurence King Publishing Ltd
361–373 City Road
London EC1V 1LR
United Kingdom
Tel: +44 20 7841 6900
Fax: +44 20 7841 6910
email: enquiries@laurenceking.com
www.laurenceking.com

A catalogue record for this book is available from the British Library.

ISBN: 978-1-85669-633-3

Design: byBOTH
Picture Research: Evi Peroulaki & Ida Riveros
Senior Editor: Melissa Danny
Copy Editor: Catherine Hooper

Printed in China

Endpapers: Front spread Photography by Clive Booth, fashion Paul Smith · Front
reverse Photography by Miguel Villalobos, fashion Boudicca · Back reverse
photography by Claire Robertson, fashion Emma Cook · Back spread photography
by Clive Booth, fashion Jonathan Saunders

Cover: Photography by Nick Knight/*Vogue* © The Condé Nast Publications Ltd ·
Fashion editor Kate Phelan · Hair by Sam McKnight · Make-up by Val Garland ·
Nails by Marian Newman · Location Park Royal Studios · Digital artwork by
Epilogue Imaging · Model Lily Donaldson · Dress by John Galliano for Dior ·
Courtesy of British *Vogue*

LAURENCE KING

Foreword ——————————————————— 6
Introduction ——————————————————— 8

Aitor Throup ——————————— ⚹ ———— 14
Alexander McQueen ——————————————— 22
Boudicca ——————————————————— 30
Burberry Prorsum ———————————————— 38
Cassette Playa ——————————————— 46
Christopher Kane ——————————————— 54
Danielle Scutt ——————————————— 62
Deryck Walker ——————————————— 66
Eley Kishimoto ——————————————— 74
Emma Cook ——————————————————— 82
Gareth Pugh ——————————————————— 90
Giles Deacon ——————————————————— 98
Hussein Chalayan —————————————— 106
John Galliano ——————————————— 114
Jonathan Saunders —————————————— 122
Julien Macdonald —————————————— 128
Louise Goldin ——————————————— 134
Luella ——————————————————— 140
Matthew Williamson ————————————— 146
Nathan Jenden ——————————————— 152
Noki ————————————————————— 158
Paul Smith ——————————————————— 164
Philip Treacy ——————————————— 172
Preen ———————————————————— 178
Stella McCartney ——————————————— 184
Stephen Jones ——————————————— 190
Vivienne Westwood —————————————— 196

Picture Credits ——————————————— 204
Acknowledgments ——————————————— 207
Designer Contacts ——————————————— 208

FOREWORD
—
NICK KNIGHT

I was recently told that that one of Britain's most important fashion houses was originally established using profits from a brothel. Whether true or not, this anecdote sets the tone for understanding British fashion. The dominant cultural, intellectual and spiritual values in post-war British society are that of the Protestant faith. Based on Puritanism, the social characteristics that are admired are hard work and honesty, modesty and straightforwardness. Set against this, fashion is representative of all the worst human values: superficiality, vulgarity and narcissism.

However, as we all know from our physics lessons at school, every force has an equal and opposite force acting against it. Rebellion against all these forces has fuelled British fashion, just as it has British music and British art. Perhaps inevitably, the dismissal by our intellectual and cultural establishment of fashion is much more pronounced than against the other mediums. Britain can feel worthy discussing and admiring art; we can understand the sense and feel the need to write about music in our Sunday papers; but to take fashion seriously, in all its ostentation and self obsession, feels just about as immoral and sinful as can be.

It is only when we realize the strength of the forces that are opposing fashion in Britain today that we truly see the strength and power in the work of designers like John Galliano, Alexander McQueen, Vivienne Westwood, Hussein Chalayan and Gareth Pugh. Then do we start to understand the incredible beauty of their work, the messages they seek to convey, and consequently their cultural importance.

Fashion is, at its most basic, the very first communication we have with each other. There has never been a society in our history as humans that has not used some form of self adornment or self decoration to communicate who we are or want to be, our social status, our political beliefs, our sexual availability. In my own experience some of the fashion designers that are in this book have taken that basic human expression and performed a unique and enviable feat, transforming it into one of the most exciting, powerful and often misunderstood forms of art ⋇⋊

INTRODUCTION

—

THE BRILLIANCE OF BRITISH FASHION

—

HYWEL DAVIES

British fashion is self-confident and brave. Critically acclaimed as a source of fresh, irreverent and fearless fashion, Britain nurtures the most dynamic and influential designers working in a global industry.

'I think British fashion is not afraid to have a voice,' says Stella McCartney, who has flown the British style flag on an international level since launching her own-name collection in 2001. 'It can be very understated and chic, but also very eclectic and eccentric at the same time.'

British fashion designers are defined by their creativity and originality. Their vigour and vivacity is never in doubt as a notorious history of innovation and a thirst for radical change has established British designers at the vanguard of inventiveness.

Creativity through adversity is a recurring theme in British fashion. 'Britain is a tough place to be,' explains Luella Bartley, who references British heritage in her collections. 'It always seems like a struggle, so when everyone has to try much harder, it brings out really strong creativity and that's how great things happen.'

Harriet Quick, Fashion Features Director of British *Vogue* supports this idea. 'London is a very expensive city to live and work in so that is a big drain on resources – however, the upside is a fascinating city with a great melting pot of cultures, a thriving creative industry and a big customer base of fashion-forward consumers.'

The culture of British Fashion thrives on new ideas – designers can be highly provocative, whereas Milan and New York tend to be more conservative platforms. 'The sheer amount of creative people in the capital raises the bar and creates a dialogue between the disciplines,' explains Quick. 'A lot of influence comes from training at CSM [Central St Martins College of Art and Design] and RCA [Royal College of Art] colleges, which emphasize expression, professionalism and doing something different and unique.'

Hussein Chalayan, who interprets a conceptual approach to fashion, shares the view that Britain's diminishing resources in fact heighten the creative output. He defines British fashion as, 'Aware, multifaceted and empowered by a lack of resources.'

Britain's rich cultural history is also integral to its fashion, according to Luella Bartley, who cites the intrinsic and dynamic link that exists between fashion and related industries. 'The fashion scene is closely linked to other creative disciplines here – art, music, film – and everybody talks and debates together,' she explains.

'The harsh judgment you get from your contemporaries means you are always being pushed,' adds Bartley, 'It all helps.' Giles Deacon supports this idea: 'You can come from an arts background or even a club background. The acceptance of people coming from different areas is much stronger in London.'

'I think British fashion's unpredictability is its charm,' explains iconic British designer John Galliano, who has taken on the fashion elite in Paris and proved that British creativity has a profound relevance. 'British fashion has history, eccentricity, uniqueness and charm.'

Every year, as the fashion shows finish their circuit in Paris, there is always copious press coverage of how good the British designers are, how productive their ideas and how uncompromising their approach to fashion. No one doubts that British designers are far-reaching and influential thinkers.

It was after all a British gent, Charles Frederick Worth, who ignited the business of fashion design in the nineteenth century. As the first fashion innovator, Worth sewed labels into the garments, established his Maison couture fashion house in Paris and set in motion the wheels of the fashion industry.

Since the growth of these couture houses in Paris there has been much discussion concerning British fashion lagging behind, which now seems more of a cottage industry than a fully cohesive industry.

Many of the big name British designers migrate to warmer climates to work for established design houses. There is a lack of government funding and recognition in Britain, which seems responsive only to the needs of the high street. It is also considered that British designers don't receive the same industry support as their competitors do in Milan, New York and the home of fashion, Paris.

It is important to consider that for the French, fashion is business. Ideas are important but they appreciate that it takes devotion to developing fabric, detail, cutting and sourcing to make a successful business. In France fashion remains an industry that supports thousands of small specialist businesses supplying everything from buttons to lace.

In Britain the infrastructure is different and unfortunately seems to be worsening. Stores often source from cheaper suppliers in Asia and the new fashion graduates push themselves to create attention-grabbing shows.

When a home-grown designer does become successful in Britain, they are often forced to decamp their catwalk shows to other fashion capitals to search for commercial success. Alexander McQueen, Luella Bartley, Matthew Williamson and Stella McCartney are all designers who have left the UK to show their collections elsewhere. Should this pattern be overhauled or accepted as the mechanics of a global industry?

British creativity cannot be disputed. Certainly fearless and avant-garde British designers are now developing a sophistication and polish that is producing covetable, even wearable clothes for international audiences. The days when London fashion only meant eccentric or bizarre fashion have long gone.

Although it is still difficult to build a business in a country where the industry is focused on mainstream clothing, relationships with Italian manufacturers and the support of international buyers looking for original talent mean that small design companies can now slowly draw out an existence.

Central to the success and abundance of British fashion designers is living and working in London. With its culturally diverse population and its attitude, London is distinct from other European cities in its multicultural modernity, which shows nowhere more clearly than in its fashion.

London street style has long inspired the world's designers. The diversity is vibrantly evident not only on the streets but informed and fed by the influential fashion design schools. Central St Martins and the Royal College of Art are internationally respected for providing the industry with bright and brave new fashion designers. These two colleges are the prestigious boot camps for fashion innovators of the future, and their success is distinct through their impressive alumni.

'Central St Martins is what makes London special,' explains Professor Louise Wilson, the MA Fashion course director at this esteemed college. 'London is a multicultural city and we attract students from all over the world. It's a creative melting pool where students find like-minded people to work with. It is here that students, sometimes for the first time in their lives, feel like they fit in. It's not easy being at St Martins. It's not glamorous, it's hard, and this makes the cream rise to the top.'

Wilson also highlights the reason why British fashion has in the past been so successful. 'We used to have a grant system which allowed people from every background to be able to come to art college, but now, will students come if they have to incur debts of over £30,000?'

The contribution that Central St Martins makes to contemporary fashion is outstanding. The majority of the designers showing at London Fashion Week have studied at this prestigious college. Recognized for producing shows that are polished, accomplished and considered, St Martins graduates are still regarded as some of the most creative and radical in the world.

'Central St Martins' track record is unmatched,' explains Mandi Lennard, a public relations agent who has nurtured many of London's designers including Gareth Pugh and Danielle Scutt. 'Every student appreciates that places on the courses are highly sought after; in as much as the tutors are passionate, the students devour the experience too.'

Lennard also recognizes that London designers work in close proximity and there is a lot of mutual support, with many sharing pattern cutters and even studio space. 'However, they could certainly benefit from more business grounding,' believes Lennard. 'Far too many of the designers I have supported left college without enough rudimentary knowledge in this area, leaving them extremely vulnerable.'

With ambitious designers leaving college in London, what follows are the fashion start-ups, all with aspirations to question and change the face of fashion. Working from a hotbed of creative exchanges, new designers present an individual and original approach to clothing. London also attracts many new international designers who choose to base themselves in a capital where creativity is encouraged and celebrated.

The British capital is perceived as somewhere that focuses on innovation and brave new ideas. As John Galliano observes, 'London is the essence of fashion. It is the most cosmopolitan city in the world. Hunger, curiosity and its eclectic, electrifying surroundings make it very inspiring.' London is where designers can build a reputation and get noticed by people from around the world. From this base they can attract customers and backers to support their future businesses. The city is still clearly revered as a place for ideas, but not always for orders.

London fashion may have established itself with a reputation as an eternal rebellious being, with designers who grow up either to move quietly on to the sidelines, or to show abroad. But now London is regarded as an influential and relevant fashion city.

Sarah Mower, fashion journalist for Style.com, believes that London Fashion Week has incredible value. 'I wouldn't miss London Fashion Week for the world. Other cities have huge self-confidence, and I wish London would accept itself as a place that promotes international new talent.'

While the art-school philosophy may encourage individuals who perhaps lack commercial sensibility to expect a spotlight when they graduate, it does allow designers to shine from an early age and define their fashion language. It is in some ways this lack of a structured industry that is actually London's strength. There is little manufacturing in the UK and designers do come and go, but the dynamic energy and unparalleled flow of ideas is inspirational and unique.

There is rarely a quiet moment in British fashion. Youthful designers who scrape together funds to put on a fashion show will always attract feverish interest in British fashion design and nourish the industry with innovative ideas. And there are now several companies that have been established in London with the aim of strengthening and promoting new fashion talent: Vauxhall Fashion Scout, Fashion Forward, New Generation, On|Off and *Blow*'s Off-Schedule Guide.

One of the first initiatives was Fashion East, which helps young designers break through at London Fashion Week by assisting them in show production, sourcing sponsorship, inviting guests and promoting their work. Designers who have benefited from the support of Fashion East include Jonathan Saunders, Danielle Scutt, Deryck Walker and Cassette Playa.

British high-street brand Topshop has sponsored the Fashion East show since 2003, and Topman have sponsored the menswear 'MAN' show since 2005. 'Our decision is quite intuitive,' explains founder and British fashion supporter Lulu Kennedy. 'It's hard to poinpoint what we look for, but we know it when we see it. The main thing is that it must feel fresh and directional.' A panel of journalists, stylists, buyers and other designers choose the participating designers and they are supported financially to present a collection.

In 2006 The Metropolitan Museum of Art in New York showed 'AngloMania: Tradition and Transgression in British Fashion' – an exhibition that celebrated British fashion from 1976 to 2006. The period was presented as a time of astounding creativity and experimentation as British fashion was defined both by historicism and the search for novelty. Britain's rich artistic traditions were applauded as a key factor influencing a wide spectrum of British designers.

Iconic British designers including Vivienne Westwood, John Galliano and Alexander McQueen have paved a creative path for future designers who are eager to present challenging new ideas for fashion. Their ideas and ideals reach beyond a select fashion audience, and their influence is felt around the world.

In 2009 the organization that oversees London Fashion Week, the British Fashion Council, celebrated 25 years of British fashion and confirmed the staying power of the industry. British fashion is now taken seriously as a source of fresh, irreverent and fearless fashion. The creativity count is soaring.

British Fashion Designers celebrates those influential designers who have defined contemporary British fashion, and those individuals who have presented their own radical ideas through clothing. Challenging preconceived ideas on fashion, these creatives are responsible for building British fashion to being honoured internationally. Their messages and aesthetic may be diverse, but their aim is the same – to define their own fashion language and present modern and fundamentally original fashion to a contemporary market. British fashion designers are brilliant 🇬🇧

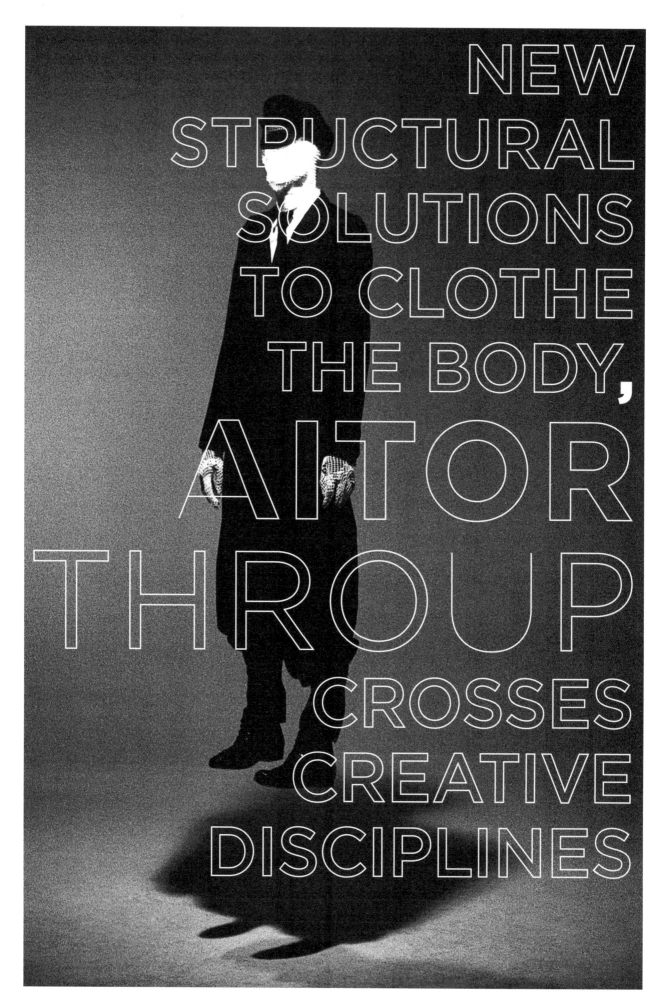

NEW STRUCTURAL SOLUTIONS TO CLOTHE THE BODY, AITOR THROUP CROSSES CREATIVE DISCIPLINES

| **p.14** | Launching simultaneously with his first on-schedule catwalk presentation as part of the MAN showcase at London Fashion Week, Throup's film collaboration with photographer Jez Tozer for SHOWstudio: 'The Funeral of New Orleans — Part One'; A/W 2007 | **p.15** | Throup's work communicates a conceptual approach to design, but still creates wearable garments. All images A/W 2007

With ideas that intersect fashion, sportswear, illustration, sculpture and film, Aitor Throup is radically changing the perception of British menswear.

Born to Argentinean parents in 1980, Aitor Throup grew up in Burnley in Lancashire. He graduated from the Royal College of Art in 2006, having received awards from Umbro, Evisu and Levi before leaving. His graduate collection, a blend of street sportswear and religious symbolism entitled 'When Football Hooligans Become Hindu Gods,' won the Fashion Collection of the Year Award at the international ITS#FIVE (International Talent Support) Fashion Awards in 2006.

Throup follows a unique design process that begins with him drawing characters, like the one opposite. These illustrations are converted into tiny sculptures, which then inform the patterns and shapes of the finished garment. During London Fashion Week in 2007, Throup launched the 'Aitor Throup Tailoring' concept, which involves the release of a single outfit every season, with the whole process becoming the finished product. So, the final package includes a copy of the original drawing, a replica of the sculpture and the finished outfit itself.

'Drawing has always been my main passion and interest,' explains Throup. 'I am interested in justifying all design features and avoiding gratuitous detailing with a focus on origin, process and innovation.'

For his first on-schedule catwalk presentation as part of the MAN menswear showcase at London Fashion Week, Throup created a film with the photographer Jez Tozer. Entitled *The Funeral of New Orleans*, the film was a response to the aftermath of Hurricane Katrina in 2005. Through his clothes, Throup told the story of how five members of a marching band protected themselves and their instruments. The presentation confirmed Throup's radical approach to both fashion design and the communication of his collections.

Although Throup thrives on his work crossing creative disciplines, his commercial sensibility has not been negated. 'I definitely see a very concise product line in the near future, with pieces extending beyond the limitations of clothing,' he enthuses. 'I want eventually to create toys, books, animations, sculptures and drawings. I want to show everything.'

How would you define British fashion? *I suppose there seems to be an inbuilt integrity in British design. Even down to student level, most people's work often has some sort of rigid inspiration or starting point. Maybe it's because of the educational system demanding a linear creative process with a clear beginning and an end. I guess there's also something about working as a designer in Britain that allows you to be 'quirky' or 'individual,' because there's an expectancy for you to be so. Maybe that's a good thing, maybe not. I'm not sure.*

| **p.16** | Throup's RCA graduate collection was a synthesis of street sportswear and religious symbolism called 'When Football Hooligans Become Hindu Gods,' 2006 | **p.17** | top left & right Black Trousers Project for Topman, 2008, inspired by the design of the M51 American Military combat trouser; bottom left Drawing for Ganesh-inspired garment for graduate collection, 2006; middle right Prototype for Stone Island Modular Anatomy jacket, A/W 2008; bottom right Process sculpture for Throup's Tailoring Concept, 2007

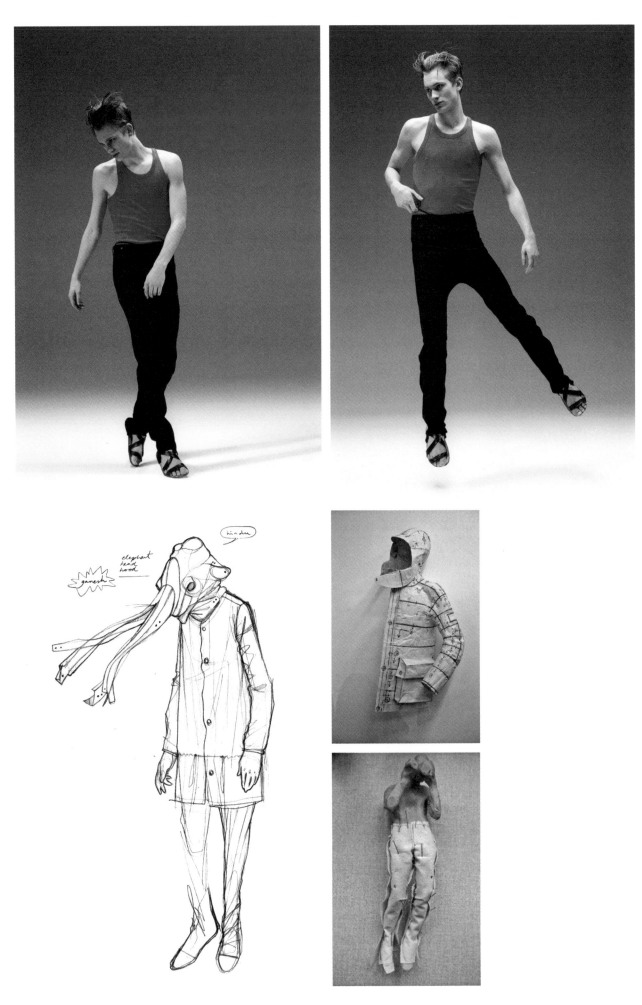

| p.18 | top middle Process sculpture for
Tailoring Concept, 2007; bottom Throup's graduate
collection, 2006; all other images Prototypes for
Stone Island Modular Anatomy jacket, A/W 2008
| p.19 | top Illustration for Throup's graduate
collection, 2006; Bottom left & right Stone
Island Articulated Anatomy, S/S 2009

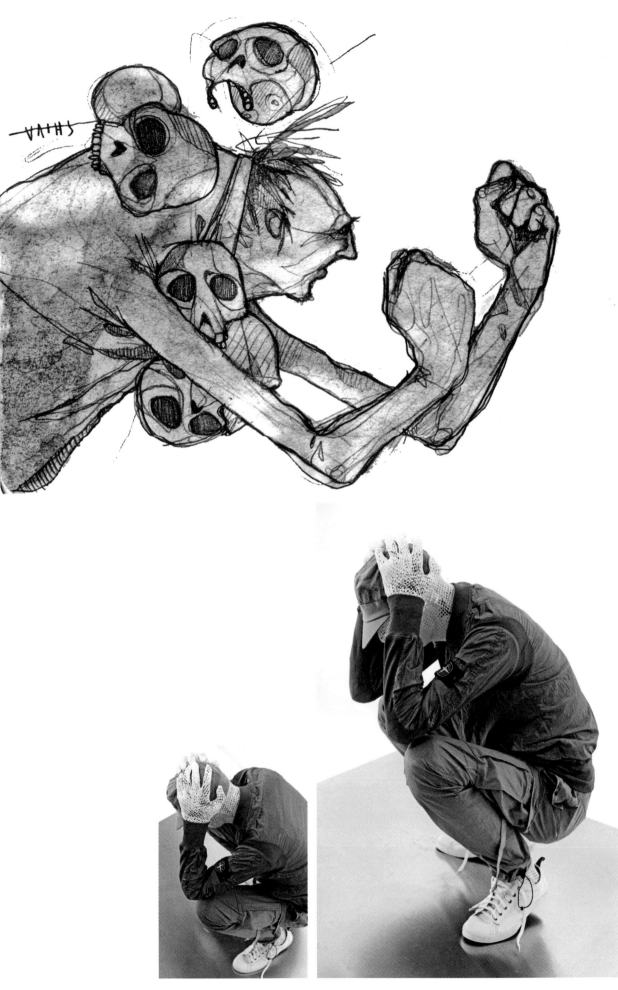

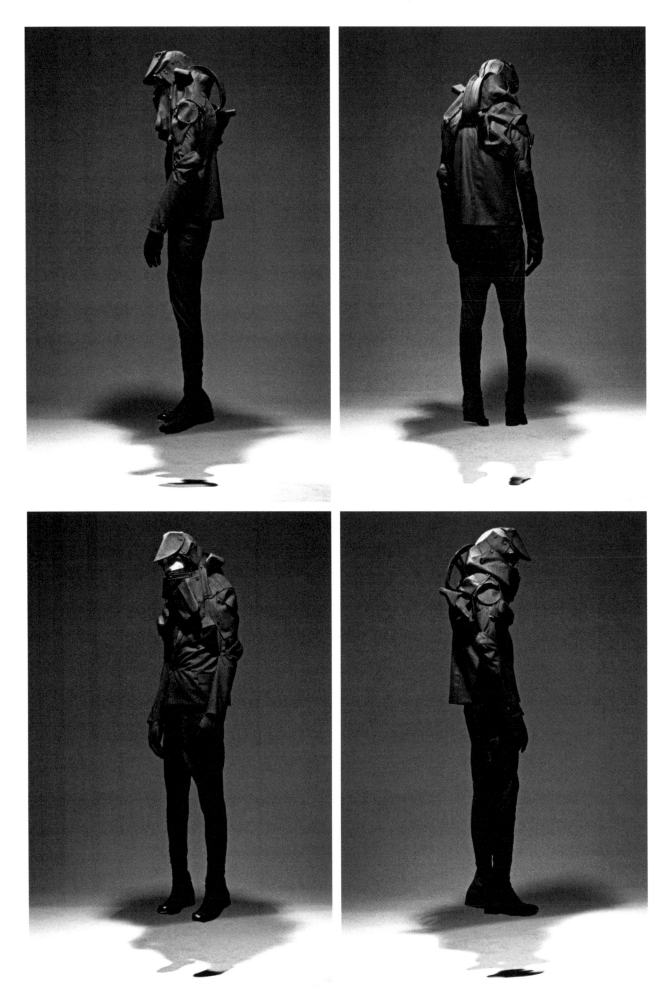

What are the pros and cons of working in London for a designer?
I guess a big benefit is that the fashion system and infrastructure is tiny. Everyone knows everyone else. That's probably a good thing because it's relatively easy for people to follow a designer's progress. Another good thing is that the weather's crap and designing is best suited to the great indoors. A rubbish thing is that London is really expensive.

Does working in Britain inform your work? *Definitely. I'd say that Burnley informs my work more than London, though. I mean, London's great, but in terms of Britishness, I'm very proud of and still inspired by my Burnley roots. I've only been living in England since 1992, when I was 12, but if I hadn't ended up here, I'm confident in saying that I would never have been involved with fashion in any way.*

Why do you think London has a reputation for creating new design talent? *I think there's a good infrastructure developed to recognize new talent (for example, graduate fashion week) in London, and the British press are always on the lookout for newly graduated talent at those events. There are also great platforms like Fashion East and MAN, and the BFC's New Gen, which offer very valuable support and exposure to key emerging designers in the early stages of their career.*

Does British fashion history ever inform your work? *Yeah, definitely. I've always been particularly attracted to the British tailoring tradition. I suppose you could look at my work as a new interpretation or approach to the same values. I also love subverting the usage and manipulation of traditional British wool fabrics. British military clothing has always been a rich source of inspiration for me and something from which I've learned a great deal.*

How do you think British designers and British fashion are regarded internationally? *I guess that during the early years of McQueen and Chalayan, London was regarded as being the most creatively rebellious and conceptual of the fashion capitals, and this has stuck. It has arguably become something different now; but on a personal level, it was what originally excited me about the prospect of coming down to London.*

Do you think there is a distinct British style? *I think there are many, particularly nowadays. There probably is, however, a distinct constant throughout all the intrinsically British styles – but it would probably take many words to attempt to define it. It just is* 🇬🇧

| **p.20** | all images 'The Funeral of New Orleans – Part One'; A/W 2007 | **p.21** | illustration by Throup, 2007. 'Drawing has always been my main passion and interest.'

FEARLESS FASHION DEFINES ALEXANDER MᶜQUEEN

Alexander McQueen is central to the creative acclaim of British fashion. With a reputation for creating shocking and challenging ideas, the 'enfant terrible' of British fashion is at the forefront of fashion innovation.

Born Lee McQueen in London in 1969, McQueen left school at 16 and undertook an apprenticeship at Savile Row tailors Anderson & Shephard and then at Gieves & Hawkes. He then worked at the theatrical costumiers Angels & Bermans, where he mastered six methods of pattern cutting, from the sixteenth-century style to the distinctive 'sharp' approach to cutting that has become his defining aesthetic.

The designer Koji Tatsuno, who also shared McQueen's expertise of British tailoring, then employed McQueen. In 1993, McQueen moved to Milan, where he worked as Romeo Gigli's design assistant. He returned to London in 1994, where he completed an MA in fashion design at Central St Martins College of Art and Design. Influential fashion-design patron Isabella Blow bought his degree collection and launched McQueen's fashion career.

McQueen's creative acclaim gave him a platform from which to launch his own label. He went on to make a name for himself with hugely provocative collections such as 'Nihilism' and 'Highland Rape.' 'British fashion is self-confident and fearless,' explains McQueen. 'It refuses to bow to commerce, thus generating a constant flow of new ideas whilst drawing on British heritage.'

Early on, McQueen's signature 'bumsters' – jeans cut just above the pubic bone to reveal the cleft of the buttocks – made their first appearance. His early presentations were revered for challenging the notion of a traditional fashion show. Intricate narratives and bold imagery united fashion, reverie, disorder and extreme beauty.

The brutally sharp approach of his collections is refined by their excellent craftsmanship, historical cut and exquisite attention to detail. McQueen's clothes are applauded for their technical wizardry and intelligent interpretation of modern fashion, making him one of the most creative designers working in London.

In less than ten years after graduating, McQueen had become one of the most respected fashion designers in the world. In October 1996, he was appointed chief designer at the French haute-couture house of Givenchy, where he worked until March 2001.

In December 2000, the Gucci Group acquired Alexander McQueen and the designer remains as creative director. Collections now include women's ready-to-wear, men's ready-to-wear, accessories, eyewear and fragrance. The Gucci Group saw the global potential of the brand, and the McQueen aesthetic was sold to the world, which included opening flagship stores in New York, London and Milan.

| **p.23** | All-in-one jumpsuit, S/S 2004 | **p.24** | top S/S 2001: a mirrored cube was revealed to be a padded cell, through which 'demented' girls wearing bandages and extraordinary dresses strutted; middle S/S 2004 was choreographed by Michael Clark; bottom A/W 2008: inspired by images of Queen Victoria and the Indian Empire | **p.25** | S/S 2008 was a tribute to Isabella Blow, the woman who discovered him, and included the theme of birds, symbolic of Blow

Launched in 2004, McQueen's menswear line adheres to the same aesthetic as the womenswear lines. 'I set out to offer a ready-to-wear collection at a Savile Row standard,' explains McQueen. 'The construction and architecture of the pieces employ the core techniques that I learned during my four-year apprenticeship on Savile Row. I have taken these traditional techniques and added modernity. I strongly believe that you must first fully understand the construction of clothes before you can begin to manipulate them in this way.'

In addition to the mainline collections, McQueen has formed partnerships with Puma in October 2005 to produce a unique exploratory footwear collection; and with Samsonite in February 2007, resulting in a cutting-edge luxury travel range. The year 2006 saw the launch of 'McQ Alexander McQueen', a denim-based ready-to-wear line that included womenswear, menswear and accessories.

Testament to his position in the fashion world, McQueen was awarded the British Designer of the Year in 1996, 1997, 2001 and 2003, and the International Designer of the Year by The Council of Fashion Designers of America (CFDA) in 2003. He was awarded a CBE in the 2003 Queen's Birthday Honours List for his services to the fashion industry, and the Fashion Director's Award 2007 for 'McQ' at the Fashion and Grooming Awards.

McQueen may have reached fashion notoriety for his challenging shows, but his contribution to British fashion is staggering. He was integral to the rise of British fashion in the early 1990s, and it is through his creative and uncompromising work that British fashion has become recognized at an international level.

Although sometimes not easy to understand, McQueen's collections have formed an international fashion brand that is both creatively and commercially acclaimed. Deviating little from his original and fearless design aesthetic, McQueen represents the very best of British fashion ⋈

| **p.26** | S/S 2001 incorporated stuffed birds | **p.27** | top left S/S 2008; top right S/S 2001; middle left S/S 2009, inspired by Charles Darwin, a zoo of stuffed endangered species flanked the catwalk, including an elephant, giraffe, polar bear and lion; middle right A/W 2001 was a sinister merry-go-round of macabre characters wearing ruffles and ancient suits; bottom A/W 2004 focused on signature McQueen shapes including jumpsuits and moulded hourglass coats

| **p.28** | top S/S 1999 finale where a machine paints a 'print' on model Shalom Harlow's simple white dress; bottom left S/S 2004; right A/W 1999 | **p.29** | top S/S 2004; middle A model performs during McQueen's choreographed show for S/S 2004; bottom A wind tunnel corridor for the A/W 2003 collection

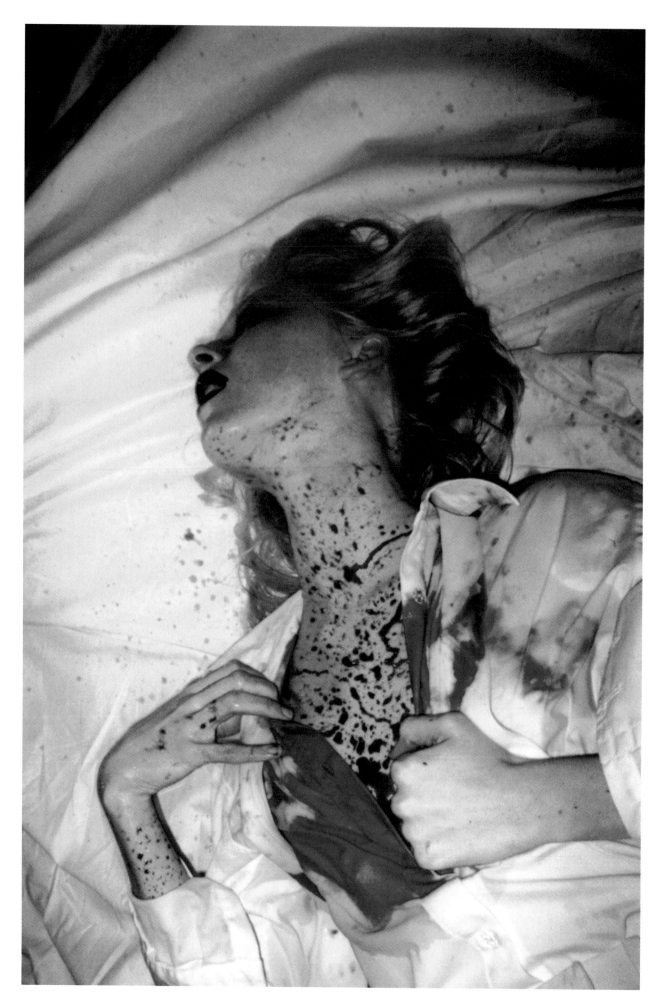

NON-CONFORMIST + CONCEPTUAL, BOUDICCA EMBODIES THE 21ST CENTURY WOMAN

'Confusion is the generator', according to London design duo Boudicca, who are respected for their conceptual approach to design and their strong political ideas. Their beautiful and strictly tailored clothes adhere to an unparalleled aesthetic that is deep, dark and cerebral.

Partners Zowie Broach and Brian Kirkby both graduated from Middlesex University and established Boudicca, named in honour of the Celtic warrior queen, in 1997. They envisioned the label as more of an art project than a fashion line, believing that the concept was similar to a conversation between two people. 'Boudicca is an exploration and documentary of ourselves and the world in which we live.'

Since then, Boudicca has communicated a strong conceptual vision that has defined contemporary cutting-edge fashion. They made their debut on the catwalk at London Fashion Week during the Autumn/Winter 2000–01 season, establishing their place as visionary British avant-garde designers. 'Boudicca is a set of tensions that climb in and out of masculine and feminine,' they explain. 'History and future tailing all thoughts, referenced on multiple levels, that when brought together form a new language that defines itself in the moment.'

Citing 'the library of imagination' as their constant inspiration, the duo approach design intellectually. 'The list of inspiration is endless as we revisit and re-weave everything we do. It is only the constant re-weaving that makes our language, and even if a small moment exists from one tiny point of reference, it will be essential for the final picture.'

Broach and Kirkby shun the fashion world, measuring their success through their fiercely loyal clientele. Boudicca trademarks include sharp tailoring, leather jackets, breath-restricting dresses, men's shirting, stiff military collars and bondage-like straps around the exterior of garments. Colours are predominantly black and a startling white.

Boudicca has shown collections in three capitals. London in the early days, New York towards the end of the ready-to-wear shows and then Paris, where they began 'the dream of further understanding the "Art of Dress" during couture week,' to which they had been invited by the Chambre Syndicale.

Collaborations have become a crucial process for the designers to instigate new ideas. 'Conversation and challenges come up when two mediums mix,' they explain. 'It is very true that at the beginning of a century you want to break up what you know by introducing something else.'

Describing their design process as 'a chaotic collision of the good, the bad and the ugly,' Boudicca are driven by a thirst to achieve a

| **p.30** | 'WODE', Boudicca's first visible fragrance, 2008 | **p.32** | collages for 'enter_Artificial Paradise', S/S 2007 | **p.33** | top left Backstage at the 'Still' C:02 Couture collection, 2008; top right 'Nature will find Her Way', S/S 2008; bottom left S/S 2008; bottom right 'Falling Rose', collage from 'Still', C:02 Couture collection, 2008

how can we go where we once went?

greater understanding of what they do. 'What propels us forward is the insatiable appetite to need more, to want to learn more, to understand more, all in the hope that maybe somewhere within we create a moment, a dress, maybe even the simplest of necklines, that amidst the emotional rendering of a real world we feel we have somehow created a change.'

Boudicca has remained true to their original vision – one that is strictly non-commercial and inherently focused on the conceptual approach to fashion. Their powerful and refined aesthetic is a unique expression of how fashion can encompass both shrewd design and politicized ideologies.

How would you define British fashion? *A history of rebellion, invention and literary cross references.*

What are the pros and cons of working in London for a designer? *London historically holds the power of the new and the anarchic, and it is this set of elements, all transient in nature, that yield negative effects and yet transform into positive ideas.*

Does working in Britain inform your work? *We are surrounded by a set of thoughts and a series of dreams, which definitely feed and influence us all from every side.*

Why do you think London has a reputation for creating new design talent? *The underdog mentality combined with an endlessly inquisitive mind, culminating in adventures of the imagination.*

How do you think British designers and British fashion are regarded internationally? *British designers are seen as original and effectively appropriate street culture.*

Do you think there is a distinct British style? *The British hate to be stylish, but possibly from an outside gaze there is a sense of Britishness. For us, what is inherently British is to be totally aware of modernity and the need for the new. We all watch an embrace of the global dialogue, of an Internet tribal exchange, which gives us less definition locally. Saying that, we are still surrounded by eccentric dress and that is what we should be most proud of. The late Isabella Blow had a wonderfully imaginative set of dress codes that inspired us, both in her language of dress and in her mindset. This is what we feel Britishness should be remembered for first of all* 🏴󠁧󠁢󠁥󠁮󠁧󠁿

| **p.34** | top left & middle 'Hidden Meanings', Preview 2009; top right & bottom left 'Nature will find Her Way', S/S 2008, included a luxurious fur coat and plenty of flowers; bottom right Sketch by Boudicca 'Butterfly Bike' | **p.35** | lace dress for 'We Sell Disguises', A/W 2003

| **p.36** | top left 'Essays'; C:03 Couture collection, 2009; top right 'The Invisible City'; A/W 2006, communicated a futuristic sensibility in their signature black and white palette with precise and masculine tailoring; bottom all three Backstage at 'Still'; C:02 Couture collection, 2008, illustrating the designers' ability to use formal tailoring and provide contrast with feminine fabrics | **p.37** | 'Essays'; C:03 Couture collection, 2009

THE FASHION SENSIBILITY OF BURBERRY IS ENHANCED BY THE PRORSUM COLLECTION

Under the guidance of creative director Christopher Bailey, Burberry Prorsum has become the beacon for global luxury brand Burberry. Fusing classic garments with a high fashion sensibility, Prorsum has re-established the label for a contemporary market.

Founder Thomas Burberry set up the company in 1856, with the first London store opening in 1891. By 1895, Burberry was making uniforms for the British army.

The now iconic signature plaid started life as the lining for trench coats, but the company owes its reputation for innovation to its patenting of gaberdine, a water-resistant material that would come to characterize Burberry's famous mac. As recognition of the company's contribution to British clothing, Queen Elizabeth II granted Burberry a Royal Warrant in 1955.

Burberry Prorsum ('forward' in Latin) was launched in 1999 as a high-end line. Christopher Bailey joined Prorsum as creative director in 2001; his mission was to breathe new life into the brand and to create a modern and luxurious clothing label.

Bailey was born in England in 1971. He graduated from the University of Westminster in 1990, and went on to study an MA in fashion at the Royal College of Art. On finishing his education, Bailey moved to New York to work as a designer for Donna Karan. In 1996, he moved to Gucci womenswear as the senior designer.

While designing at Burberry, Bailey has transformed the company into a relevant fashion brand without sacrificing any of its commercial viability. The directional Prorsum collections have afforded Burberry a platform from which to compete with other luxurious fashion labels. Defined by its classic style and shapes, Burberry produces garments in contemporary colours, modern forms and sumptuous fabrics.

Bailey is inspired by Englishness and Burberry's heritage. The Prorsum line provides clothes for the quintessential English individual, offering quirky touches on refined classic clothing.

'Outerwear is the anchor and the starting point of everything we do, it is the heart of our rich 153-year-old history,' explains Bailey. 'The Burberry trench coat is iconic, unique, functional, ageless and timeless.' Under Bailey's creative design direction, the trench coat – Burberry's famous signature piece – is re-imagined and updated every season.

The Prorsum brand is known for its sophistication and fresh approach. Bailey has created an internationally recognized and dynamic luxury fashion label. Perfectly balancing the creative and the commercial, Bailey has charmed his customers and created a credible force in British fashion.

| p.39 | The painter L. S. Lowry inspired the luxurious A/W 2008 collection for Burberry Prorsum, which featured tiered feathers and suede sequins | p.40 | top Buckle detail from the famous Burberry trench coat; middle both 'Garden Girls' collection, S/S 2009, inspired by Bailey's own garden in Yorkshire; bottom all three A/W 2008 | p.41 | A/W 2009 was influenced by Bill Brandt, the photographer who captured the austere years after World War II

| **p.42** | Christopher Bailey understands how accessories are integral to the Burberry Prorsum collections. For A/W 2008 quirky hats and coats were on show | **p.43** | The 'Garden Girls' S/S 2009 collection fused Bailey's signature super-deluxe trenches with garments that were dip-dyed and crinkled to create a 'worn' look

Bailey's success at Burberry led him to be awarded Designer of the Year at the British Fashion Awards in 2005 and cemented his position as an innovator of contemporary British fashion.

How does being British inform your work at Burberry? *I'm British and Burberry is as British as they come. But I wanted to know everything when I was approached for the role: who was this Thomas Burberry who so brilliantly founded the company when he was just 21? As a brand and as a company, we always look at the foundations; we have the most incredible rich history and unrivaled archives that are always the starting point, and then we look at ways to innovate these incredible style staples, like the classic Burberry trench coat, an icon known the world over, and how that can be modernized, reinterpreted, but always in the Burberry spirit.*

Does Burberry define Britishness? *Burberry has always been a real British institution. I come from Yorkshire in the north of England and as a young boy Burberry was to me a British icon. Burberry is part of the culture and the DNA of the UK, like Big Ben, The Houses of Parliament and Piccadilly Circus, to name but a few. My father and grandfather owned Burberry trench coats and they had this incredible quality about them, they could be worn with anything and still look elegant but in a natural and unforced way. Burberry outerwear has such a timeless quality, and I wear pieces today that I have had for many years, long before I worked here.*

Does working in Britain inform your work? *I love London. It has a lot of energy and is rich with culture and tradition as well as irreverence. I work and live in London during the week, but Yorkshire will always be my home. I am at my most serene when I'm there at my house with my family and my oldest friends, the people I have known since I was at school.*

Does British fashion history ever inform your work? *That is the beauty of Burberry – it reflects England and our history because it has been a part of so many different eras, 153 years of history. The queen wears a trench coat; Sid Vicious of The Sex Pistols wore a trench coat. Explorers love it as much as businessmen and women, rock stars, city dwellers and farmers* 🇬🇧

| **p.44** | For the A/W 2008 collection, autumn leaves were strewn on the catwalk | **p.45** | the late artist and filmmaker Derek Jarman informed the vintage-looking menswear S/S 2009 collection, which Bailey called 'Crumpled Classics', shown in the top three images; bottom both A/W 2008

THE CARTOON COUTURE OF CASSETTE PLAYA SUBVERTS SPORTS + STREETWEAR

Designed by Carri Mundane, Cassette Playa is renowned for its kaleidoscopic casual uniform that has been appropriated by London's club kids. Inspired by real and virtual worlds, Mundane has an energetic vision that is inherently graphic and modern.

Mundane studied fashion design at the University of Westminster and on graduation immediately launched her collection at a London nightclub. Her clothes presented a youthful spirit that captured a new energy in menswear, and have since been bought by influential stores The Pineal Eye in London and Side by Side in Tokyo.

Mundane's fashion language is described as 'graphic, future, positive and primal' and refers to computer games, virtual reality and the media. By responding to popular culture, Mundane's clothing concepts defined and dressed the nu-rave dance scene that manifested itself in London's clubs.

Although Mundane's clothes are presented on men, she describes her garments as 'mixed wear' – essentially menswear that can also be worn by girls. Ettore Sottsass, Keith Haring and Versace are among her design icons and with bright, often fluorescent, colours and prints as central to her aesthetic, signature pieces include baggy tracksuits, tie-dye T-shirts and oversized shorts.

Street fashion, according to Mundane, is fashion in its purest form. 'It's about defining your identity. It's both a personal expression and tribal and it's about defining yourself as a group.' The designer believes that it is important for her to immerse herself in street culture to ultimately influence it. 'I've always been interested in subcultures because I see them as tribes,' she explains. 'But I've always been something of an outsider and never fitted in anywhere enough to say I belong to anything in particular. But that's how I like it. I wouldn't want to choose alliance when I'm drawn to so many different things. I never felt part of any particular subculture or school but I was always proud to be British.'

Cassette Playa explores how clothes can react with the wearer's senses and reflects controversial references such as psychedelic drug culture and raves. Mundane says, 'I reference a lot of other cultures in my work but my own identity and background has definitely informed Cassette Playa.' Contemporary methods of communication – the Internet, email and texting – have also hugely influenced her collections.

For Mundane, the most rewarding part of her work is meeting and working with artists whom she respects, and also seeing her designs being worn by real people. 'There's a lot of depth and concept behind my work,' she says. 'But I want everyone to be able to get it. It should be instant to read. The people and artists who I admire the most, for example Keith Haring, had a complete and complex world that was clear in its identity and message. I want to make clothes men want to wear – not just ideas.'

| **p.46** | S/S 2007 'L.S.I.' collection communicates the designer's vibrant approach to contemporary fashion | **p.48** | a showpiece from the L.S.I. collection inspired by computer games | **p.49** | the 'Future Primative' collection, S/S 2008, was based on an imaginative apocalyptic city where skaters and Amazonian hunting rituals existed

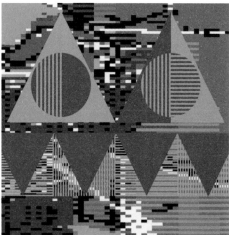

Mundane also successfully works as a fashion stylist and contributes her colourful vision to magazines such as *i-D*, *Dazed & Confused* and *Super Super.* Aiming to redefine luxury for a new generation, she is rooted in her quest to understand communication and culture. 'Ultimately I want every process, every part of my business to be conditioned by this quest,' she explains. 'And, on a personal level, I want to be fearless in my design because I want my men to be fearless.'

How would you define British fashion? *Knowledge of tradition, individuality and a fearless creativity.*

What are the pros and cons of working in London for a designer? *London is a multicultural, historic and modern city. It is these cultural fusions and divisions, characters, subcultures and layered narratives that I love. This is my inspiration. There is a family, if a little dysfunctional, of other designers around you. There is competition but everyone is individual. There is respect and support for each other.*

Does working in Britain inform your work? *I think globally but I am very proud to be British. My work explores exactly what it means to be British now. For me it's a complex identity built up of tradition and cultural differences but with an overriding sense of pride and strength. I take a lot of inspiration from street, sports and youth culture. I respect the UK's part in that heritage (football, firms, casuals to rave and dub, grime culture) and I take inspiration from what is happening on the streets and in youth culture now.*

Why do you think London has a reputation for creating new design talent? *UK designers are fearless. The city, especially its music, art, clubs and street culture, is all the fuel you need.*

Does British fashion history ever inform your work? *I'm sure it does indirectly, but my references and inspirations are rarely purely fashion.*

Do you think there is a distinct British style? *British style is all about attitude. From dandies to rude boys, it's all about a smartness that's worn and subverted. I'm interested in aspiration dressing. Class is a defining element of British style and fashion.*

Which other British designers do you admire and why? *Kim Jones because he redefined menswear for a new generation. His vision is the future, intelligent and sexy. Vivienne Westwood is the ultimate in what I said before – a clash of tradition and individuality, fearless creativity* ⚔

| p.50 | bottom left A bold, graphic black and white outfit from the 'L.S.I.' collection, S/S 2007; all digital prints on silk or jersey, clockwise from top left 'Dozzee Warrior'; 'Crack'd Out Emo Duck'; 'Gif Face'; 'Teeth Eyes'; 'Pyramid Monster' | p.51 | S/S 2007 shows a toxic colour uniform of patterns and graphic shapes in the luxury street and sportswear | p.52 | top both from *ID* Horror Issue shoot, June 2006; bottom S/S 2007 | p.53 | S/S 2008

BODY CON + EDGY, CHRISTOPHER KANE DESIGNS BEAUTI**FULL**Y REFINED CLOTHES

Glaswegian Christopher Kane produces bright, sexy and dynamic clothes. Creatively fusing fabric, colour and print, Kane is at the vanguard of British fashion design.

Christopher Kane was born in 1982 near Motherwell in North Lanarkshire. Inspired from an early age by John Galliano's creativity, he studied fashion at London's Central St Martins College of Art and Design. His 2006 graduate show received praise from the press and Donatella Versace immediately offered him a consultancy role at Versace.

In September 2006, Kane showed his first independent show at London Fashion Week. Skintight pieces referenced the work of Gianni Versace, Azzedine Alaïa and Hervé Léger. Bands of neon elastic were wrapped around the body, and stretch-lace minidresses in fuchsia, purple, midnight blue and aqua were decorated with ruffles and brass rings. Kane works in tandem with his sister, Tammy, who is his collaborator and business partner. 'Collaborations are good to make you see things outside of the fashion box,' states Kane. 'They offer opportunities to learn and experience new things.'

With a design philosophy of 'working hard and trying to do something interesting', Kane has captured the modern essence of London fashion. Citing Versace and Iris Apfel as inspirational design figures, Kane finds it harder to define his own aesthetic. 'I want women to feel really special in my designs, but my ideas on aesthetic change like the weather.'

His work is often inspired by memories. 'From watching films to drawing, no matter what I make it always ends up reminding me of something or someone from my childhood.' Kane's design process involves drawing, then working on a mannequin and then on the body to edit the garments. 'Sometimes I don't draw and just come up with a textile idea that will take you somewhere else,' he explains. 'There isn't a blueprint for it and I think I do things backwards, but what works for me might not work for someone else.'

Kane finds it hard to be wholly satisfied with his work. 'I always want to do more and more. That has a lot to do with limited resources here in London. It can be tough to have designs executed exactly how I had imagined when drawing them. It can be heartbreaking; if it isn't perfection, then I don't want it.' But on the other side of the coin, according to Kane, imperfections can be the perfect result to get his creativity flowing. 'It all depends on the collection and what overall aesthetic, look and sensibility you are trying to achieve and portray.'

For Kane, the fashion show is the most exhilarating part of his work. 'You get to see for the first time all the models lined up with the complete collection on,' he enthuses. 'It takes about four months to make a collection so it feels like a landmark to get to that stage.'

| **p.55** | Kane's graduate MA collection from Central St Martins in 2006 defined his edgy and forward approach to fashion | **p.56** | top right A/W 2006; top left & bottom left A/W 2008 collection signalled a changed in direction — the clothes were less sexy and more refined; bottom right Drawing by Kane | **p.57** | A/W 2008 demonstrated the designer's expertise in handling delicate fabrics

| **p.58** | top A/W 2008; bottom left S/S 2009; middle & bottom right Kane's A/W 2009 collection focused on grey and black clothes, styled with flat lace-up shoes, and his organza dresses showed careful crafting | **p.59** | A/W 2007 collection used tough black and oxblood leather with burnt orange, scarlet and emerald velvet

How would you define British fashion? *Innovative, fresh and energetic. Young and up-and-coming designers spring to mind when I think of British fashion.*

What are the pros and cons of working in London for a designer? *The benefits of working here in London are the support you receive from the British Fashion Council and Topshop – without them it would be terribly difficult to fund two catwalks shows a year. Also, just being in London is good for a designer; there is so much to absorb visually. Most of my time is spent in Hackney where I live and where my studio is. The negative aspects facing designers in London is that there are very few factories left, it's a struggle to bring ideas to life due to the limited skills and resources here.*

Does working in Britain inform your work? *Yes it does. I like the diversity of London – I like the posh versus ghetto feel that London has.*

Why do you think London has a reputation for creating new design talent? *I think Central St Martins has a lot to do with this. Louise Wilson has taught most of the biggest names in fashion. My dream was to move away from Scotland and to come to London as soon as I left school to go to Central St Martins. London is the capital with so much going on – every borough is different.*

Does British fashion history ever inform your work? *I think as a designer you absorb all sorts of pieces of history. I like to pick at things, but mostly I like to look forward.*

How do you think British designers and British fashion are regarded internationally? *I think we have an excellent international rep for being creative.*

Do you think there is a distinct British style? *Yes of course, if we are talking about new designers then I would say it is a place to find a new creative energy.*

Which other British designers do you admire and why? *Charles Worth for inventing couture. Vivienne Westwood for being so amazing, she gave us punk in the 1970s and is still changing the way we think about dressing. I love her for that. John Galliano for making me want to go to Central St Martins and for being a true genius. There are so many, like Alexander McQueen, who have contributed so much to fashion* ⧉⧉

| **p.60** | A/W 2008 | **p.61** | top left, top right & bottom right Ruffles, washed-out denim and snakeskin were masterfully brought together in his S/S 2008 collection; middle both and bottom left Details of Kane's elaborate fabric from the A/W 2008 collection

CLOTHES FIT TO **FIGHT** IN BY DANIELLE SCUTT

Fuelled by the power-dressing of the 1980s, Danielle Scutt's clothes are visceral and vivacious. Designing with a philosophy to celebrate the empowerment of women, Scutt's vision is dynamic and uncompromisingly fierce.

Scutt graduated from Central St Martins College of Art and Design in 2005. While at college she won the Chloé Award for best designer and was also awarded the Lancôme Award for Modern Femininity.

Describing her design philosophy as 'design for now', Scutt launched her label at London Fashion Week in 2006. Her first collection immediately presented a powerful and challenging portrayal of women. Inspired by the hedonistic female characteristics of power and sexuality, Scutt's clothes are ruthlessly dynamic and edgy.

Key reference points for Scutt are 'women, Helmut Newton, power, sexual attraction and Prince,' and she lists Rudi Gernreich, Claire McCardell and Paloma Picasso as her definitive design icons. Scutt creates confident clothes that are incredibly alluring with a touch of rock and roll attitude.

Defined by her love of very close-fitting garments, Scutt has crafted an idiosyncratic look. Canvas fitted jackets, coats with puff sleeves, pleated pencil skirts, high-waisted narrow trousers, spray-on catsuits and skintight silk jersey leotards are just some of her trademark pieces.

Scutt's strictly tailored collections clearly present an assertive and modern attitude. She admits to 'feeling sick from excitement about a design or idea,' and constantly strives for excellence: 'Surely every designer is a perfectionist?'

How would you define British fashion? *Testing the boundaries of acceptable taste.*

What are the pros and cons of working in London for a designer? *It takes two hours to get to work every day and my studio is like a youth detention centre – the block is full of ex-offenders trying to be florists and carpenters. The studio is cheap.*

Why do you think London has a reputation for creating new design talent? *Because of Professor Louise Wilson.*

Does British fashion history ever inform your work? *I prefer American right now, but maybe in the future.*

How do you think British designers and British fashion are regarded internationally? *I imagine they are not highly regarded judging by the poor international press and buyer attendance at London Fashion Week*

| **p.62** | A/W 2008 | **p.64** | A/W 2008 described by Scutt as having an effortless style: relaxed and eclectic, strong and feminine, unpretentious and uncontrived | **p.65** | top five images S/S 2009, inspired by a vintage Norma Kamali dress, Andy Warhol's *Interview* covers and Helmut Newton shoots; bottom left A/W 2008; bottom right both S/S 2008, models shown as feminist power vixens in patent bondage-strapped animal prints and 1980s-inspired swimwear

DERYCK WALKER CREATES SHARP + PRECISE CLOTHING

Sharp tailoring characterizes Deryck Walker's work. With a sense of masculinity in his womenswear collections and femininity in his menswear garments, Walker successfully employs androgyny to present contemporary interpretations of classic garments.

Deryck Walker was born in Scotland and studied Fashion and Textiles at the Glasgow School of Fine Art. After college, Walker relocated to London to work for designers including Boudicca, Robert Cary-Williams and Andrew Groves. Following a time in Milan working for Versace, Walker returned to the UK to launch his menswear collection in 2004. The successful debut collection was sold in Dover Street Market, London, and then in 2008 Walker presented his first womenswear collection.

Crisp shirts, precise workmanship and a muted colour palette of black, navy and white are integral elements of Walker's style and highlight his artistry. Subtle design details, such as sharp knife pleats on an A-line skirt, are also characteristic of his contemporary take on fashion design.

How would you define your aesthetic? *I always like a man to be a man but I do like a little bit of the feminine. I think that it contrasts, making the man look even more handsome and the same for women. There is nothing sexier than a woman wearing masculine tailoring.*

Do you have a design philosophy? *To be coherent and respect the balance of what you are working with. Sometimes it's best not to overwork things or go against the form that you are working on.*

What reference points do you often revisit? *I revisit most of the things that I do when cutting, like the sculptural element. It's something that can be developed to create new shape, which I can then bring in to the clothes. Francis Bacon's art is something that I constantly look at, too.*

Do you have design icons? *I am not too sure that they are just 'design' icons, but my style icons are Francis Bacon, Vivienne Westwood, Sade, Suzanne Vega, John Deakin and my mother.*

How would you describe your design process? *This can change every season, it all depends what I am working on. Sometimes I start by playing around with patterns such as windmills, which are my signature shape.*

How important are collaborations within your work? *Collaborations are very important to me. I feel that bringing in other elements can make your collection really explode, often resulting in a total shift from what you were originally thinking.*

Are you ever completely satisfied or are you a perfectionist? *As a designer, I don't think you are ever 100% satisfied; that's what*

| **p.67** | Shot for *Pop* magazine, these pleated shorts and 3D box shirt were styled by Andrew Davis as an outfit from Walker's second MAN show called 'Oracle', S/S 2007 | **p.68** | Walker's S/S 2008 menswear collection demonstrates the designer's innovative approach to materials | **p.69** | 'Oracle' also celebrated Walker's signature colours of black, white and navy with a focus on shirting, trousers and a variety of jackets

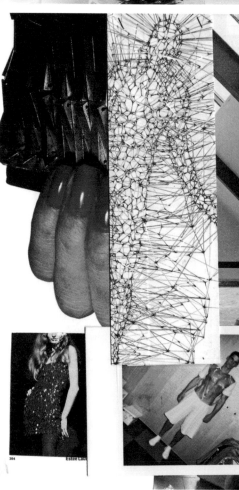

| **p.70** | top three images S/S 2009; bottom left Moodboard for the S/S 2008 collection; bottom right three images S/S 2007 included perspex panels on shirts and jackets and even see-through shirts | **p.71** | top left S/S 2009; top right 'Machine' collection, S/S 2006; bottom left Interpretation of a sculpture made for the Reindeer Restaurant, London, and constructed of over 1000 windmills, his trademark symbol; bottom right both A/W 2009

it is all about for me – pushing what you do so that someday in your head it will be perfect.

What is the most rewarding part of what you do? *Seeing it come together and the opportunities that come your way. So far I have been very lucky, but have worked hard for it. Also, being in the studio working with my team is amazing and being able to be this creative is beautiful.*

How can you be modern in fashion? *Being modern is more about an attitude, not just what is worn and how you carry yourself. I really enjoy dressing for winter – this is very inspiring for me as I come from Scotland where winter is hard. Layering up a winter look is a very creative process that inspires my collection for the coming seasons.*

How would you define British fashion? *British fashion, for me, is always a reflection on what is happening at a certain time. Almost like some sort of revolt, like punk for example. Pissed-off kids, DIY fashion, making music and fashion out of rubbish, creating something totally new.*

What are the pros and cons of working in London for a designer? *London is becoming so expensive, and if you are young and trying to start up a label with little cash it is a nightmare. But on the flip side of that, people tend to be more creative when they are skint. Another great aspect of London is that you meet all the other dreamers who flock here from all over the world. Cross-referencing these cultures makes London a very inspiring place to be.*

Does British fashion history ever inform your work? *I really love the 1940s and 1950s. They were really hard times but with a huge shift in youth culture. It must have been great if you were coming into your teens as you would not really have been affected by the war and you would have embraced this new social change.*

How do you think British designers and British fashion are regarded internationally? *I think that some might regard us as a bit wacky.*

Do you think there is a distinct British style? *When I think of British fashion I think of Savile Row, being very smart and elegant. Then there are all the different looks that come every decade: 1970s punk, 1980s power-dressing and 1990s nihilism. It is always a distinctive look that goes against the grain.*

Which other British designers do you admire and why? *Vivienne Westwood, for me, has always been the best. I loved how she struggled and never lost her edge. I feel that without her we would never have seen a lot of the designers that came after her. She is what British fashion is all about* ✻

| **p.72** | S/S 2009 | **p.73** | top three images Walker collaborated with Harris Tweed and presented his collection in a gentleman's club in Paris; bottom S/S 2008 men's collection focused on crisp tailoring with Mondrian-style colour blocks. The colour palette was kept quite bare, with mostly white and grey and splashes of yellow and baby blue

DYNAMIC + PLAYFUL, ELEY KISHIMOTO ARE **PRINT** MAVERICKS

'We are surface decorators and the world has many surfaces to cover,' says the design duo Eley Kishimoto, whose quirky graphic prints adorn not just clothes but crockery, furniture, wallpaper, luggage, trainers, lingerie, cars and sunglasses.

Wakako Kishimoto was born in Sapporo, Japan, in 1965 and graduated from Central St Martins College of Art and Design in 1992 with a BA in fashion and print. Mark Eley was born in Bridgend, Wales, in 1968 and graduated from Brighton Polytechnic in 1990. Uniting the contrasting British and Japanese sensibilities, the couple have developed a brand that has its roots in the culture and environment of London.

Eley Kishimoto was founded in 1992 when they began designing prints for Joe Casely-Hayford, Hussein Chalayan, Alexander McQueen, Jil Sander, Versace, Yves Saint Laurent, Louis Vuitton and Clements Ribeiro. Their approach to printed textiles in fashion is unique and their distinctive graphic prints are highly respected.

In 1995, Eley Kishimoto produced their first collection, entitled 'Rainwear' for the season Autumn/Winter 1996–97. They presented their first on-schedule show during London Fashion Week for their Autumn/Winter 2001–2002 line.

The duo tries to produce work that is clear in its aims, simple in its execution and full of creative flair. Describing their aesthetic as 'pretty, hard, rigid, cheeky, awkward and printed,' the designers try to avoid seasonal trends, instead using fashion to communicate with diverse audiences.

A retrospective exhibition of Eley Kishimoto's work was held at the Victoria & Albert Museum in London in 2002, and in 2003 they opened a shop in London. Spring 2005 heralded the first Eley Kishimoto-Ellesse collection – part of a three-season deal that saw the label explore sportswear. In 2008, they were appointed as creative directors of French-based fashion house Cacharel.

Eley Kishimoto are designers who have defined and pushed print in fashion by using colour to create clothing that is both young and innovative. Their unique approach to fashion has been revered internationally as being progressive and modern. Fusing humour, craft skills and an understanding of form and colour, the design team produces radical clothing.

How would you define British fashion? *Varied, traditionally traditional, contemporarily experimental and generally tribal. When there was a textile industry there was the opportunity to really define British fashion, but in the present day and with globalization and offshore manufacturing we hold on to the notion of British style, which is an amalgamation of past ideals, incorporated creativity and designer high-street derivatives.*

| **p.74** | For S/S 2008 Kishimoto were inspired by a village fete, using rosettes, bows and candy colours to create a young and vibrant collection | **p.76** | bangles with signature Flash pattern | **p.77** | top left, middle centre & bottom S/S 2006, 'Cosmic Dolls on Earth' collection; top right sunglasses by Linda Farrow; middle left signature Flash print; bottom right Animal Camo print from A/W 2004

What are the pros and cons of working in London for a designer?
On the positive side, there are established infrastructures that allow college leavers to create a label and put it into the global fashion arena without much investment. Like-minded people support us. Some of the best globally recognized magazines, stylists and photographers live, create and play in London, which must influence creativity. College interns are in abundance, all willing to work for free in the hope of gaining a job at the end. Pub culture, gallery culture, club culture, drug culture and pop culture.

The negative aspects include the fact that London doesn't seem to go anywhere really business-wise. Not many people travel to London for the shows, as the biannual schedule is too long to get them to go to all four capitals. It is expensive to live and work in London when your production runs are maybe 5000 pieces per season. There is no support from the banks as they see fashion as an unreliable entity. There is too much emphasis on design while at school only for you to realize that you will be picking up pins for the next few years. All the manufacturing in the UK has gone.

Does working in Britain inform your work? *Of course. This is where we live, and it is only natural that our local environment, friends and family as well as the wider community are imbued within our work.*

Why do you think London has a reputation for creating new design talent? *I think it was the nature of the subcultures that were an extension of the music from the 1950s and 1960s, and now it is the number of graduates from supposedly the best art schools in the world. If you look at the links between these two poles, you will find a reason why young creatives have been so prevalent in the UK.*

Does British fashion history ever inform your work? *Not really, but we started our business focusing on cloth and manufacturing that can be executed in the UK, so through this maybe there are traces of British history.*

How do you think British designers and British fashion are regarded internationally? *With creative flair but not much business prowess.*

Which other British designers do you admire and why? *Paul Smith for building an identity and a global following; Vivienne Westwood for being herself. McQueen for allowing us to work alongside him and witness that there are still opportunities to be competitive on a global scale* 🏴

| **p.78** | Kishimoto's S/S 2008 collection created prints with names such as Super Zebra, Loopy Lawn and Glitzy Ditzy | **p.79** | S/S 2008

| **p.80** | top left Entitled 'Little Devils'; the S/S 2009 collection was inspired by the magical world of a children's playground; top right Flash Eastpak collaboration, S/S 2009; middle left & centre S/S 2009; middle right EK3 print; bottom Kishimoto showroom, S/S 2007 | **p.81** | Silk printed party coat in Domino Butterfly print for 'Butterfly Brigades Nightmare'; S/S 2004

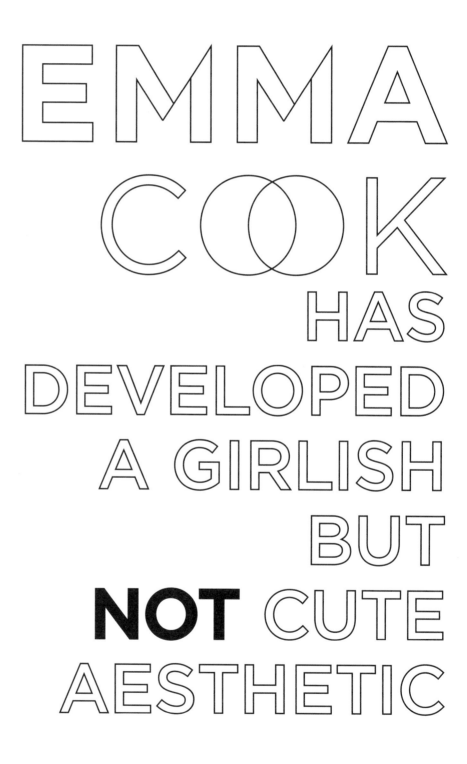

EMMA COOK HAS DEVELOPED A GIRLISH BUT **NOT** CUTE AESTHETIC

Emma Cook's clothes combine quirky femininity with exquisite detailing, rich textures and retro styling. An advocate of using directional prints, Cook evokes a sense of history and unique character in her garments.

Born in Manchester in 1975, Emma Cook studied textile design at the University of Brighton, before undertaking an MA in womenswear at Central St Martins College of Art and Design. Her 1999 graduation collection was acclaimed by the British press and focused on her unique attention to detail that has come to define her work.

Cook went to work for Martine Sitbon in Paris, and then for Ghost, Liberty and Ruffo. She started her own collection after winning a Vidal Sassoon Young Talent Award, which enabled her to produce a London Fashion Week show for Spring/Summer 2001.

Although Cook's collections are often described as girlish, they are always very graphic with strong construction techniques. Recurrent themes include art nouveau references and natural elements such as foliage, birds and images of animals. 'Make sure it's flattering,' explains Cook on her design philosophy. 'It doesn't matter how modern a dress is, no girl wants to wear it if it makes her legs look chunky.' Cook's design identity is based on individuality and her collections are not marked by seasons, but are designed to be worn over and over again.

Focused on finding the story behind the clothes, Cook names each collection after her imaginary muse Susan. The character has assumed many guises from Joan of Arc to Barbarella. For her Spring 2004 presentation, Cook was inspired by 'old-fashioned ideas about futurism, Rodchenko, the constructivists and 1920s statues of ladies.' The pieces had machine-cog motifs, prints of butterflies and flowers and deco-inspired leather inserts.

The Spring/Summer 2009 collection revisited Cook's love of animal motifs with the idea of the 'Twenties meets Safari'. Zebra-emblazoned prints and birds adorned fringed dresses and harem pants, realizing Cook's ability to produce quirky but wearable collections. Transparent rain macs were decorated with Swarovski crystals and dresses and pencil skirts were zipped from the hem all the way to the waist.

By developing a girlish but not cute aesthetic, Cook ensures that her collections present original twists on contemporary fashion. Materials are always handcrafted, and print and embellishment is key, as is working collaboratively. 'I have always worked with my friend and stylist Cathy Edwards. We work very closely, and also my friend, set designer Shona Heath,' states Cook. 'It's really good to get so many female opinions.'

The most rewarding part of her job is seeing people wearing and enjoying her clothes, but the design process always brings new

| p.83 | A/W 2008 showed the designer's refined skills in tailoring and included military-inspired hats and coats | p.84 | top three images Cook created a film to present her A/W 2007 collection that included camel smock-dresses and clean-cut cream tops; bottom right Detail of raffia showpiece for S/S 2007; left three images A/W 2003 offered a sleek and modern collection of appliqué leather A-line skirts, tunics and jumpsuits | p.85 | S/S 2007

challenges. 'I wouldn't describe myself as a perfectionist,' she explains. 'But I am never satisfied.'

Cook may be constantly striving for perfection, but her fashion collections have represented a distinct and important aspect of the London fashion scene since 2000. Catalyzing the wave of new cool British fashion designers, Cook is an essential part of London Fashion Week. Her signature vision of feminine but continually edgy fashion has developed into a highly respected brand with a clear identity.

How would you define British fashion? *It's more experimental than that of other countries.*

What are the pros and cons of working in London for a designer? *I think you get a better team in London. I have spent time working in New York, Milan and Paris, and there is definitely more passion and enthusiasm here.*

Does working in Britain inform your work? *I am happiest here, with my friends and family. That makes my work better.*

Why do you think London has a reputation for creating new design talent? *St Martins has a lot to do with it, but there are more possibilities here. In Milan or New York you can't just leave college with nothing but a good idea and some talented mates and show a collection at fashion week.*

Does British fashion history ever inform your work? *Yes, all fashion history does. I think it's really important to know inside out what has happened previously in fashion to be a good designer.*

How do you think British designers and British fashion are regarded internationally? *Not as we would like to be. I think Britain is seen as a place to discover new talent but not a place for big business.*

Which other British designers do you admire and why? *All of those who stay in business*

I **p.86** I Dresses are a signature of Cook's collections, shown here at A/W 2008
I **p.87** I Close-ups reveal the delicate fabrics, beading, embroidery and print all brought together in A/W 2008

| **p.88** | top left A/W 2002; top right Runway looks from A/W 2008; bottom left A dropped-waist dress is heavily fringed for Cook's S/S 2009 collection based on the 1920s; bottom right both S/S 2008 | **p.89** | S/S 2008 shows the designer's quirky and original experimentation with print

STARK + FUTURISTIC GARETH PUGH PRESENTS **WAR**RIOR WOMEN

One of London's most exciting and avant-garde designers, Gareth Pugh produces immaculately made garments that are constructed in dramatic and provocative styles. He challenges current attitudes towards clothing and design.

Pugh has received global recognition for his contemporary approach to fashion. Born in Sunderland, he studied on the art foundation course at the City of Sunderland College before going on to Central St Martins College of Art and Design, graduating in 2003.

Describing his clothes as 'strict and dark,' Pugh often focuses on opposites: black and white, masculine and feminine, good and bad, right and wrong. Admitting he does not have a design philosophy, he instead does 'whatever it takes to get the job done'.

In using a variety of materials, including inflated PVC, perspex and latex, Pugh creates a dramatic futuristic vision of fashion. His design process is immediate. 'I'll get to the studio and decide what I want to do,' he explains. 'Some things take a lot longer than others to get out, but generally things happen very organically. Things grow into other things, and I end up with something that doesn't at all resemble what I started to make, but something that still makes sense.'

Pugh assisted Rick Owens on a work placement at luxury furrier Revillon, where he met Michelle Lamy, the Parisian fashion consultant, and in 2006 Lamy became Pugh's official backer. The union signalled a more luxurious direction in Pugh's work, with the introduction of cashmere, leather and mink to his collections.

In 2005, Pugh debuted at London Fashion Week, off-schedule as part of Fashion East's group show. Following Fashion East in the same year, his illuminated finale piece was worn by model Jade Parfitt in HSBC's global advertising campaign.

As part of ON | OFF in 2006, Pugh received New Generation support from Topshop, which was also awarded to him for his next show later that year. In 2007, he headlined at the MID_E Festival to celebrate the Guggenheim Museum's tenth anniversary in Bilbao, Spain. He was then crowned Young Designer of the Year at the ELLE Style Awards.

Pugh works closely with Kylie Minogue on her tours, the photographer Nick Knight/SHOWstudio, Swarovski, Moët & Chandon, Kopenhagen Fur and MAC Cosmetics. His work has been exhibited at The Costume Institute at The Metropolitan Museum of Art in New York, and at The Museum at FIT (Fashion Institute of Technology) in New York. Pugh's designs are stocked in stores in Japan, New York and London.

In 2008, Pugh won the prestigious ANDAM award, which enabled him to show in Paris for the first time and also allowed him to

pp.90-91 | Pugh's A/W 2008 collection focused on exaggerated shoulders through 3-D shapes | p.92 | The S/S 2007 runway was covered with cotton and inflated into a billowing river | p.93 | all images S/S 2007: outrageous figures, their bodies and faces sprouting 3-D geometric shapes, wore coats made from patchworks of black-and-white vinyl, survival-blanket silver foil and plastic which was blown up with air

| **p.94** | Pugh often uses unorthodox materials, like this goat-hair outfit, A/W 2008 | **p.95** | top left A/W 2007 included outstandingly constructed and intricately pieced-together striped garments; top right Sculptural and challenging clothes for A/W 2008; bottom Dramatic red clothes in S/S 2006, an unusual colour for Pugh

develop his business. At 150,000 Euros, it is the largest fashion prize in the world.

Pugh maintains a perfectionist attitude. 'I'm never satisfied,' he says. 'I think it's important for me to maintain a distinct sense of dissatisfaction with whatever I do, otherwise why would I ever need or want to do anything else? With each season comes the perpetual search for the unobtainable – the perfect collection.'

With a distinct design aesthetic, Pugh has become a highlight of the international fashion calendar. He has wowed London with the most dramatic shows and challenging clothing and has brought the creativity of London to international recognition.

How would you define British fashion? *Raw, creative and modern.*

What are the pros and cons of working in London for a designer? *London seems to be a place where a lot of very talented and inspiring young designers migrate towards. There is good and bad to this – there are lots of opportunities for young designers to start showing in London, but there aren't enough resources available to continue this support for each designer after they have established themselves.*

Does working in Britain inform your work? *Who and what is around me always inspire me. London is certainly a vast resource.*

Why do you think London has a reputation for creating new design talent? *The constant want and need for something new, which is the driving force that surges though fashion and keeps it all moving forwards.*

Does British fashion history ever inform your work? *It's not necessarily something that I look at and reference in any literal sense. I think it's important to do something modern, even if it's referential of the past, to push it into a new space, and to make it relevant for today, tomorrow even.*

How do you think British designers and British fashion are regarded internationally? *Personally, I find that there is a lot of support. People are intrigued to know what is coming out of London. British designers are very well represented internationally and this really gives a solid heritage to both contribute to and live up to.*

Do you think there is a distinct British style? *I think there is a distinct British designer: someone who does what feels right and someone who believes in what they do.*

Which other British designers do you admire and why? *I admire anyone who can do what they love and make a living out of it* 🇬🇧

| **p.96** | top & middle three A/W 2008; bottom For his first show in Paris, Pugh's S/S 2009 collection explored the designer's signature pieces, including exaggerated shoulders and nipped waists | **p.97** | A/W 2008

GILES DEACON

MERGES COUTURE SENSIBILITIES **WITH** BRITISH WIT

Giles Deacon's vision combines craft sensibilities with quirky elements of British wit. Describing his garments as 'clothes that don't blend into the background,' Deacon fuses eclectic references to create eminently wearable dresses and signature statement pieces.

Originally from Cumbria, Giles Deacon studied at London's St Martins College of Art and Design. After graduating in 1992, he worked for radical French designer Jean-Charles de Castelbajac, and from 1998 until 2002, Deacon was employed as a designer for luxury Italian brand Bottega Veneta, owned by the Gucci Group. His debut collection for the brand was progressively hard-edged, raising Deacon's profile as a future fashion name to watch.

After a stint designing Gucci womenswear in Milan, Deacon presented his first, own-name collection during London Fashion Week in 2004. Deacon's debut show was styled by friend and influential editor of *Pop* magazine Katie Grand, with music by Steve Mackey of Pulp and lighting by John Akehurst. Deacon employed supermodels Karen Elson, Eva Herzigova and Nadja Auermann and established himself as a major force in British fashion. 'We had the choice to show anywhere in the world,' explains Deacon. 'I have lived in other places, but London has really informed me where we are now as a company.' By showing in London, Deacon knew he would have a good platform for his designs, along with more press attention. The show was an immediate success and was featured in American, British, Japanese, Italian and French *Vogue*, as well as *Harper's Bazaar*. High-end British stores Harvey Nichols, Liberty and Selfridges all purchased the debut collection.

Deacon describes his clothes as 'well made and expensive. The clothes have a sort of "thing". It's hard to describe, but I like the fact that I can't describe it, but I know it when I see it.' His often eccentric clothes are not created within themed collections. Instead, he prefers to 'be spontaneous and go with gut instinct,' incorporating lots of contrasting elements into his pieces. Everything Deacon creates is a reflection of his own taste, he believes. Some of his designs in recent collections have included ostrich-feather bodies, 3-D dancing-skeleton prints and S&M-themed kaftans.

In 2004, Deacon was crowned Best New Designer at the British Fashion Awards and Best New Designer by *ELLE* magazine in 2005. In 2006, he was awarded British Designer of the Year.

For Deacon, London is a place that is more immediately accepting of new designers and talent than other fashion capitals. 'Milan and Paris are a lot more difficult to crack. Milan has a strong manufacturing heritage and Paris has a strong couture base.' According to Deacon, London focuses on being progressive and design led: 'It is important for an identity purpose but I don't really like being pigeonholed,' he states. 'I choose to live and work in London. And, as long as the association has nothing to do with a twee Britishness that's about teacups then I am happy.' He believes that a designer

| **p.99** | A/W 2006 focused on bold stripes, dots, gigantic leopard spots and fluorescent pattern described by Deacon as 'Femme fatale in a gothic disco' | **p.100** | A/W 2008, | **p.101** | all photographs A/W 2008, inspired by *The Masque of the Red Death* horror movie; bottom right Sketch by Deacon

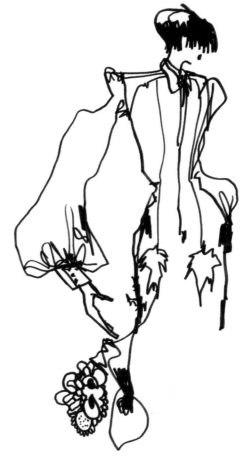

can come from an arts background or even a club background because London accepts people coming from different areas.

For his Autumn/Winter 2008–09 collection, Deacon was inspired by the Hammer Horror film *The Masque of the Red Death* (1964), an adaptation of Edgar Allan Poe's story of the same name about 'people partying in a castle with everyone dying outside.' Deacon used Marabou feathers, helmets, studs, rivets and even chain mail to magnificent effect.

Admitting that some of his clothes 'can be subversive,' Deacon says he strives to make obtainable clothing. 'It's not a difficult aesthetic; I design dresses that will make women look and feel a million dollars, with the added bonuses of edginess and sex appeal.'

In addition to expanding the ready-to-wear collection, Deacon introduced accessories in a two-season collaboration with Mulberry. He also works with high-street retailer New Look to design New Look Gold, and has breathed new life into the British tailoring brand Daks.

Aside from fashion design, Deacon is a renowned illustrator whose work has appeared in *Interview*, *The Face*, *Pop*, *i-D*, *Dutch* and *Arena Homme Plus*, and has formed part of the print design in his ready-to-wear collections. He is fascinated by animals and insects, and motifs of apes, bees, scorpions and lizards often crop up on his clothes. He explains, 'I am fascinated with studying the general shape and dimensions of everyday objects.' Deacon's illustrative work was part of a group show at the Roma Roma Roma gallery in New York in 2006.

The Giles Deacon brand has established itself as a key fixture of London Fashion Week. His high-octane ultra-sexy presentations are often touted as the show to see. The toast of the British fashion capital, Deacon, for all his idiosyncratic ways, has continually delivered exciting and experimental fashion. As a designer at the forefront of creative fashion design, Deacon has a unique sense of humour that never detracts from the creation of innovative and beautiful clothing. In his own words, 'I like to be in the real world' ⧓

| **p.102** | top left A/W 2008; bottom left both A/W 2009, a collection that revisited his previous signature pieces in an attempt to recapture the fun he had while studying at Central St Martins; right Printed silk duchess 'Razor' dress, S/S 2007 | **p.103** | A/W 2008

HUSSEIN CHALAYAN IS FUELLED BY **NEW** TECHNOLOGY, SCIENCE + RADICAL MATERIALS

Defining his aesthetic as 'a gap between fantasy and reality,' Hussein Chalayan is well known for his radical use of materials, meticulous pattern cutting and forward-thinking approach to new technology. As a beacon of innovation in British fashion, Chalayan identifies and questions contemporary approaches to clothing.

Hussein Chalayan was born in Nicosia, Cyprus, in 1970. He graduated from London's Central St Martins College of Art and Design in 1993. Describing his design philosophy as 'a thesis,' Chalayan has always thrived on a conceptual approach to fashion design. His degree collection consisted of silk dresses that he had buried and later exhumed from his garden. The collection was an immediate success and was bought by the prestigious Browns boutique in London, launching him on the international fashion stage.

Establishing his label in 1994, Chalayan won the Absolut Design Award in 1995 and was named British Designer of the Year in both 1999 and 2000. Chalayan is inspired by architectural theories, science and technology, and he revisits certain reference points, including anthropology, history, immigration and institutions. His design icons include Elsa Schiaparelli and Pierre Cardin. Using film, installation and sculptural form, Chalayan explores the perceptions and realities of modern life. He describes his design process as very personal: 'The process is really for me to be able to achieve my goal. That may or may not mean anything for others.'

While Chalayan's work is presented at fashion shows, it is also exhibited in art galleries and museums worldwide, including London's Victoria & Albert Museum, The Kyoto Costume Institute in Japan, Paris's Musée de la Mode et du Textile and The Design Council at Grand Central Terminal in New York. In 2002, Chalayan began showing his collections in Paris and launched his menswear range. In 2004, his diffusion line, Chalayan by Hussein Chalayan, was introduced.

Chalayan has been directing short films since 2003, and represented Turkey in the 2005 Venice Biennale with *Absent Presence*, featuring Tilda Swinton. In 2005, The Groninger Museum in The Netherlands hosted a ten-year retrospective of his work, and he had several pieces exhibited in the 'Anglomania' exhibition at the New York Metropolitan Museum of Modern Art in 2006. Chalayan has worked as the creative director of Asprey, as a designer for TSE New York and as a guest designer for London retailers Topshop and Marks & Spencer. He has collaborated with Swarovski on several of his fashion shows, and in 2008 he was appointed as creative director of Pu.

For his Spring/Summer 2007 show, Chalayan created a range of motion dresses, which morphed in front of the audience to express 111 years of fashion. The collection propelled the viewer through fashion history. The commentary at the heart of the show focused on the contemporary habit of recycling 'vintage' yet, at the same time, embraced high technology.

| **p.106** | For his A/W 2000 collection, a model stepped inside a table, lifted it up and it transformed into a wooden skirt | **p.108** | A/W 2007 included a dress made out of LED lights | **p.109** | all images A/W 2008 finale, featuring mechanical dresses that sent out moving spots of light configured to symbolize the Big-Bang beginning of the universe

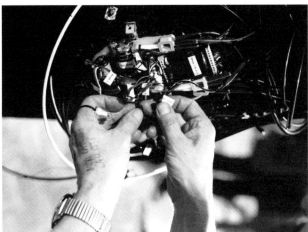

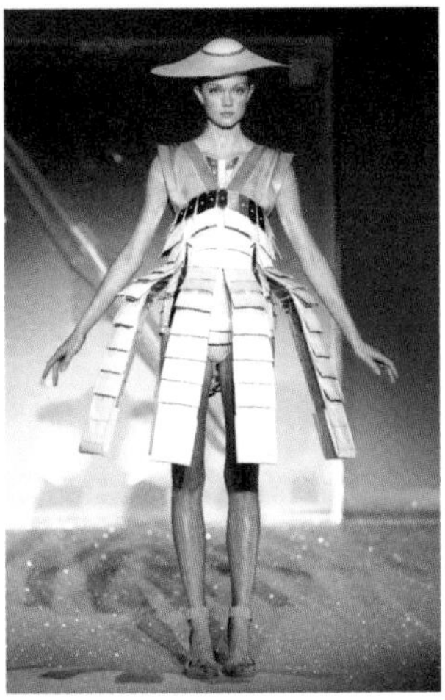

| **p.110** | top S/S 2001 saw girls holding tiny mallets proceeded to break to pieces their companions' dresses; middle A/W 2007; bottom left A/W 1998; bottom right S/S 2000 | **p.111** | Chalayan's S/S 2007 collection involved clothes that changed and morphed into new garments

Moving garments have become a defining aspect of Chalayan's work. For his Autumn/Winter 2000 show, staged at Sadler's Wells Theatre, London (see overleaf), the audience compared the presentation with performance art. The stage set consisted of modernist furniture: four chairs and a circular coffee table. Throughout the show, models wearing his signature refined pieces moved around the furniture. For the finale, a model approached the table, removed an inner wood ring from it and stepped into the table, transforming it into a skirt. The covers from the chairs were then removed, unfolded and became dresses.

Uniting theatrics with radical clothing design, Chalayan is known as one of the industry's most intellectual designers. For his Autumn/Winter 1998 collection, he dressed models in traditional Muslim headdresses but left their bodies naked. His presentation outraged the Muslim community, but attracted the attention of the press.

Challenging preconceived ideas of what clothing is, should and can be, Chalayan was integral to the explosion of British fashion in the early 1990s. His radical ideas on fashion and presentation propelled British designers into the international limelight and showed London as a formidable source for producing unrivalled talent and innovative designers.

In 2006, Chalayan was awarded an MBE in the Queen's Birthday Honours List, and his work continues to explore the possibilities of fashion design. For Chalayan, the most rewarding part of his work is still 'to turn a dream into a reality.'

How would you define British fashion? *Aware, multifaceted and empowered by a lack of resources.*

What are the pros and cons of working in London for a designer? *London becomes a noticeable platform for a designer in the beginning. However, longevity certainly comes from forces outside the UK.*

Does working in Britain inform your work? *Yes, it's the New York of Europe, culturally and ethnically. On the other hand, the lack of resources can actually make me more resourceful at times.*

Why do you think London has a reputation for creating new design talent? *The standard of the colleges, the multinational reality and the Anglo-Saxon tolerance.*

How do you think British designers are regarded internationally? *They are regarded with great respect, but more from a point of view of drama and not always as serious businesses*

| **p.112** | The dramatic A/W 2003 collection
| **p.113** | left three images Presentation at Sadler's Wells Theatre, London, A/W 2000, where models in shift dresses put on chair covers, the last stepping inside a table that opened out into a wooden dress; right top & bottom A pink moulded plastic dress was opened up by a remote control panel held by a young boy to reveal a froth of pink tulle underneath, S/S 2000

OUTRAGEOUS IMAGINATIVE, JOHN GALLIANO ADORES A FASHION FANTASY

'I am on a quest for perfection,' declares iconic designer John Galliano. With a wildly romantic and often outrageous approach to fashion, Galliano explores eclectic historical references and presents brilliantly beautiful clothes.

Juan Carlos Antonio Galliano was born in 1960 in Gibraltar. His family moved to London in 1966, where Galliano went on to study fashion at Central St Martins. His celebrated graduation collection of 1984, called *'Les Incroyables'* and inspired by the French Revolution, was bought by Joan Burstein of Browns boutique and marked the start of Galliano's illustrious career.

'I think you have to be curious and have the courage of your own convictions. Keep it fresh and keep it exciting – that is the key,' explains Galliano, whose fervent desire to innovate is significant in his success. Galliano presented fashion shows in London until 1992, after which he decided to move Paris where he could reach a wider and more international fashion audience. He won the British Designer of the Year Award in 1988, 1994, 1995 and 1997. In 1995, Galliano became the designer for the House of Givenchy and after only two seasons was offered one of the most prestigious positions in fashion: as designer for the House of Christian Dior.

Galliano's signature style is distinct. 'It is very English,' he states. 'It is a combination of moods, muses and moments. It is high-tech romance with a twist.' England and all things English constantly inspire Galliano, 'be it literature, art or music. I love the street culture, the uniforms, Savile Row, I love it all.' Known for building his collections on characters that drive a narrative, Galliano has a long list of design icons: 'Men or women. Dead or alive. I have many; they are the mood, the colour and the core to creation.'

Collaborations are also important to the designer: 'Friendships and partnerships are invigorating, inspiring and enriching.' Milliner Stephen Jones, set designer Michael Howells and DJ Jeremy Healey are all key collaborators. Galliano describes his creative process as exciting, 'I start with the research and from this I build the muse, the idea, tell a story, develop a character, a look and then a collection.'

Every aspect of his work drives Galliano, who says, 'The people I meet, work with, the research, the creative process, the show, the clients, I love all of it.' According to the designer, a garment is complete when it is perfect and there is nothing to add, subtract or change. 'When it is fully fashioned, styled and fitted and being worn, then it works.'

And so what is Galliano's definitive design philosophy? 'My role is to seduce.'

| **p.115** | A dress decorated with jewels for S/S 2006 | **p.116** | top left & bottom S/S 2008, a show inspired by Argentina, with 1920s flouncing tulle and chiffon; top right A/W 2005 | **p.117** | S/S 2000

John Galliano

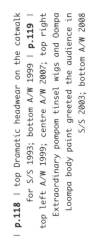

| **p.118** | top Dramatic headwear on the catwalk for S/S 1993; bottom A/W 1999 | **p.119** | top left A/W 1999; centre A/W 2007; top right Extraordinary pompom tinsel wigs and Oompa Loompa body paint greeted the audience in S/S 2003; bottom A/W 2008

How would you define British fashion? *Unique. Exciting. Individual. Fearless.*

What are the pros and cons of working in London for a designer? *Anything is possible, anything goes – but sadly there aren't always the investors to support you.*

Does working in Britain inform your work? *I work in Paris, but visit London as much as I can! London is vibrant, eclectic, exciting and original. There is nowhere else like it.*

Why do you think London has a reputation for creating new design talent? *Hunger, curiosity and its eclectic, electrifying surroundings. London is the most cosmopolitan city in the world!*

Does British fashion history ever inform your work? *Always. From Savile Row to the street. From Worth to the newest name. British fashion is very inspiring, very special, in England and beyond. It was, after all, an Englishman who founded the Chambre Syndicale de la Haute Couture in Paris!*

How do you think British designers and British fashion are regarded internationally? *I think Britain produces some of the most exciting names in fashion. British designers have a world-wide reputation – talent should be nurtured and treasured.*

Do you think there is a distinct British style? *I think its unpredictability is its charm. It has history, eccentricity, uniqueness and charm.*

Which British designers do you admire and why? *From Charles Worth to Ossie Clark and from Tommy Nutter to my team. I like rebels, revolutionaries, people that have affected and inspired me* 🇬🇧

| p.120 | A/W 2008 showcased patterned knits and flimsy layers under thick jackets, with a rich colour palette of burgundys, russets and navies, interspersed with coral, orange and turquoise | p.121 | A/W 2008

JONATHAN SAUNDERS DESIGNS WITH SILK-SCREEN COLOUR + CHIC

'I design for the modern woman who is independent in the way she thinks and the way she dresses. My designs are defined by a clean, sculptural yet feminine aesthetic.' Jonathan Saunders's clothes celebrate an expertise in print techniques and colour.

Scottish Jonathan Saunders graduated from Glasgow School of Art in 1999. He went on to study at Central St Martins College of Art and Design and graduated in 2002 with an MA in printed textiles, winning the covetable Lancôme Colour Designs Awards. In 2003, he showed his debut collection at London Fashion Week, and in 2008, he began showing his collections at New York Fashion Week.

Renowned for his intelligent approach to fashion and his contemporary take on fashion design, Saunders successfully coordinates designing his own-name label alongside consulting for some of the largest fashion houses in Europe. In 2008, Saunders was signed up as the creative director of prestigious Italian luxury brand Pollini.

Traditional silk-screen printing techniques are fundamental to Saunders's work. He has created a specific process of engineering prints designed around individual pattern pieces. The particular shape of each item of clothing influences the design of its print. Rather than having a standard print that is repeated throughout a collection, Saunders has used as many as 20 silk screens on one garment and up to 20 prints within a single collection. As the fashion industry moves towards digital printing techniques, Saunders has created a point of difference in his work.

Saunders cites Elsa Schiaparelli as an inspirational design icon: 'She truly combined art with fashion, without becoming pretentious or over-intellectualizing clothing. Also Helmut Lang, because I think that both he and Melanie Ward defined what focusing a brand is all about. They demonstrated how fashion can cross over into many different fields but with a common focus.' He goes on to say, 'I admire those who are receptive to the influence of the people and the environment that surrounds them.' He appreciates other creatives who have forged their own path, irrespective of trends, and have a unique design aesthetic that communicates a clear vision.

Research, for Saunders, is the most enjoyable part of his design process and he finds it exciting to explore techniques and discover images from fine art to design. 'Architecture has a lot of influence on my work and print continues to be integral, without dominating my designs.' Collaborations are also relevant in Saunders's work, and in 2008, he designed the costumes for the Siobhan Davies Dance Company. 'When two fields complement each other well, you create a new viewpoint on your work.'

Driven by the end result, Saunders believes that 'different pieces from each collection inspire different women'. He feels his customer has an appreciation of minimal elegance, following fashion, but not led by it. Admitting that it is difficult to be completely satisfied with

| **pp.122-123** | For his S/S 2008 collection, Saunders used colour-blocking, banding and ribbed knitwear, as well as a distinctive 1980s Italian palette of dulled-pastel pinks, yellows, blues and beige, set against black | **p.124** | A/W 2004, a collection demonstrating his skill in manipulating surface design by engineering his patterns to flow over the body | **p.125** | top three A/W 2004; bottom S/S 2008

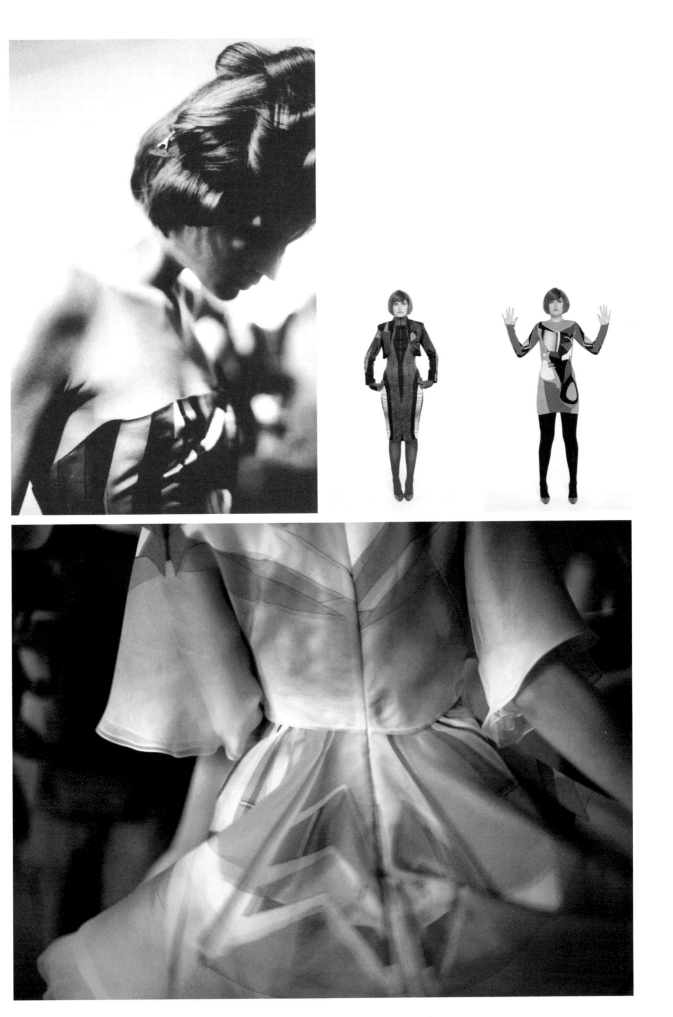

his work, Saunders explains, 'It's all a matter of degree. I like my work to be perfect, but there's always a point where commercial demands takes over.'

For Saunders, the current fashion industry is dynamic, energetic and constantly changing, and he believes that for clothes to be relevant they have to reflect this diversity. 'With our exposure to mass media, we absorb immeasurable amounts of information. In this first decade of the twenty-first century I do not think we have had a defined image such as in the 1960s, 1970s and 1980s. Instead, contemporary fashion is simply defined by how eclectic and diverse it is.'

Saunders's signature graphic prints and sophisticated use of kaleidoscopic colour have earned him international respect. His structural design, clean lines, cinched waists and fluid layers encapsulate a distinctive craftsmanship that combines futurism and quality.

What are the pros and cons of working in London for a designer? *Commercially, becoming recognized on the international stage can be a slow process, but London also provides a wealth of inspiration that's unrivalled for a designer.*

Does working in Britain inform your work? *Of course, the diversity of London and its artistic influences are constantly inspiring. I take these influences when designing for my own label Jonathan Saunders or for Pollini, where I am creative director.*

Why do you think London has a reputation for creating new design talent? *The fashion colleges, including Central St Martins, are internationally recognized as being among the best in the world. This means eyes are on London when it comes to spotting new talent.*

Does British fashion history ever inform your work? *Yes, fashion history always provides interesting reference points, but this is not limited to only British influences.*

How do you think British designers and British fashion are regarded internationally? *The increased presence of global buyers from the top boutiques and the most respected international press at the London shows is testament to the authority of British style.*

Do you think there is a distinct British style? *The definition of British style is that it is not distinct; instead it is eclectic and unique and has created an identity as being this* ⚒

| **p.126** | top S/S 2008; middle & right S/S 2005, where Saunders referenced the stark geometry of the German art-house aesthetic, melding bold lines, circles and a palette of monochromes, teal, blue, orange and yellow into simple shapes; bottom left A/W 2007 | **p.127** | For A/W 2007 dresses were constructed from narrow panels of royal blue and black

JULIEN MACDONALD LOVES HIGH-OCTANE **GLAM**OUR + SPARKLE

Described as the 'The King of Glamour', Julien Macdonald always puts on fashion shows that are a glitterati feast. With a vision that is uncompromisingly shiny and sparkly, Macdonald has made a name for himself as a designer who embodies glamorous fashion.

Born in Wales in 1972, Macdonald attended Cardiff School of Art and Design, where he discovered his fascination with textile design. He went on to study fashion textiles at the University of Brighton and started experimenting with new techniques in knitwear, realizing his full potential by the time he graduated from the Royal College of Art in 1996.

Macdonald's graduation show caught the attention of the fashion press, and Karl Lagerfeld had already commissioned him to design knitwear for Chanel. 'I am passionate about knitwear, which is where I started,' explains Macdonald. 'And it is never far, even now, from the surface of my work.'

In 1997, Macdonald created his own label and debuted at London Fashion Week. According to the designer, his garments are 'glamorous, sexy, luxurious, high-octane, powerful and liberating'. With a design philosophy founded on celebrating femininity, Macdonald has captured the notion of dazzling grown-up clothes.

'Seeing a woman look and feel fabulous, feminine and sexy in my clothes' is the reason why he designs, citing the female body as the key reference point in his work. 'It is so sensuous, varied and inspirational,' he says. As a result of his enticing and daring clothes, in 2001 and 2003 Macdonald won the British Glamour Award.

Loud prints, sequins, diamanté, crystals and sparkly fabrics are all signature components for Macdonald, who also endorses the use of fur. 'Fur is a luxury item. I make women look glamorous and sexy. If you want to look conservative you don't buy Julien Macdonald. If you are an international traveller who likes fabulous things like diamonds and expensive clothes, you are attracted to Julien Macdonald. Almost 60 per cent of my business is catering for the Russian market and my biggest sales are fur. Russian women demand fur coats and they won't wear anything else because it's so cold and they want to look fashionable.'

Named head designer for venerable Parisian fashion house Givenchy in 2001, Macdonald replaced Alexander McQueen. He put his own spin on the traditional couture house and stayed in the position for three years before returning to London to focus on his own label.

Christian Dior, Chanel, Karl Lagerfeld and Yves Saint Laurent are design icons for Macdonald. 'They are all great fashion designers that have achieved iconic status,' he explains. 'I always keep an open mind and try to learn something new every day. You just need to be observant and give women what they want. That helps you to stay in touch with fashion.'

| p.129 | A/W 2009 presented all-beaded and bejewelled floor-length dresses that shimmered and sparkled down the catwalk | p.130 | top both & bottom left Glamorous eveningwear in luxurious fabrics, A/W 2009; bottom middle A/W 2008; bottom right Macdonald often uses fur, as here on the catwalk for S/S 2007 | p.131 | A/W 2009

Macdonald's ability to design show-stopping barely there numbers is clearly appreciated by the rich and famous. He has dressed many celebrities and they often grace his catwalks, but it is the clothes that drive his ambition. 'I always want to do more and be better and as soon as one collection is designed, I am thinking about how to improve for the next one.'

In 2004, Macdonald launched a more affordable range with high-street chain Debenhams. In 2006, he was awarded an OBE in the Queen's Birthday Honours List for his services to fashion. He has now cemented his position as a designer who has brought energy and vibrant fashion to the international circuit.

How would you define British fashion? *Creative, directional, eccentric, innovative and provocative.*

What are the pros and cons for a designer working in London? *London is uniquely inspirational and stimulating for designers as it is a melting pot of so many different cultures. However, many of the biggest fashion houses, therefore the best jobs, are based outside the UK. That's a big challenge for British designers.*

Does working in Britain inform your work? *London is my base and many of my ideas come from London. However, I travel extensively and my work reflects many influences from around the world, as well as books, theatre, art and design.*

Why do you think London has a reputation for creating new design talent? *Londoners are encouraged to express themselves creatively from an early age, and the city is very liberal and multicultured. That is all great for nurturing young talent.*

Does British fashion history ever inform your work? *Definitely, there's always an underlying Englishness in my work. I love English eccentrics such as Edith Sitwell, Oscar Wilde and Isabella Blow. They all had such strong and individual personalities.*

Do you think there is a distinct British style? *There have been many distinctive and unforgettable British styles from Savile Row to punk rock and I'm sure there will be many more.*

Which other British designers do you admire and why? *Vivienne Westwood because she truly defined a style and the whole history of her label is a wonderful British story. Sir Paul Smith for championing Englishness in design. And, I also admire the work of Ossie Clark, Charles James and Jean Muir* 🏴󠁧󠁢󠁥󠁮󠁧󠁿

| **p.132** | Short skirts and yet more fur for A/W 2009 | **p.133** | top both images Sparkling floor-length dresses in A/W 2009; bottom The runway was draped in Persian rugs for a S/S 2006 collection that featured the designer's signature use of sparkle and sequins

PUSHING KNITWEAR FORWARD, KNITTING INNOVATION IS CRUCIAL TO LOUISE GOLDIN

Pioneering a new era in knitwear, Louise Goldin describes her clothes as 'futuristic, feminine, innovative and constructed'. Ambitiously refining and modernizing her craft, Goldin holds a powerful place in contemporary fashion knitwear.

Louise Goldin graduated from Central St Martins College of Art and Design with a distinction in fashion knitwear in 2005. Her graduate collection was ordered exclusively by Selfridges in London, and was shown at London Fashion Week in February 2005 as part of Central St Martins' MA show.

Combining highly technical knitwear with new and unique techniques, Goldin produces radical work. 'Never be afraid. Be brave,' believes Goldin, whose impressive body-contouring forms and garments are very different from traditional knitwear and challenge people's preconceptions of a craft-based medium.

By mixing different yarns, such as lurex and cashmere, Goldin focuses on developing new technologies. Between her studio in London, where she designs and researches the collections, and her factory in Italy, she investigates new ways of approaching and working with knitwear. 'I am drawn to architecture, armour, science and technology,' explains Goldin. 'However, I try to perceive these ideas in different ways each season. I am not at the stage where I revisit one particular topic or visual imagery. I like to step in to the unknown and create something different.'

Goldin's design process is intense: 'As soon as one collection is finished, the next one begins by ordering yarns, selecting colours and making the fabric – this is a long process, which takes a lot of development.' Watching the creative process evolve from research, to design, to toiles and patterns, to making the fabrics and to realizing a collection is very satisfying for Goldin. 'Seeing the collection on the runway as a presentation to journalists, buyers, friends and family is rewarding,' she says. 'Seeing women wearing my pieces is exceptionally rewarding and fulfilling.'

Goldin affirms that as a young designer there are always things to learn, better decisions to make and the possibility of refining the product to a higher standard. 'There are always areas of both the business and the creative side that can and should be improved as time goes on,' she explains.

The complex nature of Goldin's work has elevated knitwear to a high-fashion arena and has proved that its potential is vast. Widely credited with bringing knitwear into the twenty-first century, Goldin creates modern and young clothes that are original and dynamic.

| **p.134** | A/W 2009 | **p.136** | A/W 2009 saw Goldin present her industrial and futuristic vision through knitwear | **p.137** | S/S 2008 showed Goldin's skills with cut and pattern, presenting a colourful collection that included tight, bright dresses and dynamic swimwear

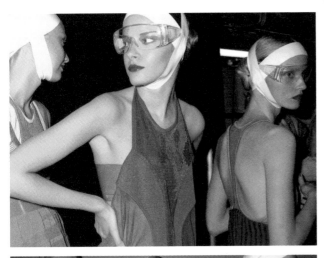

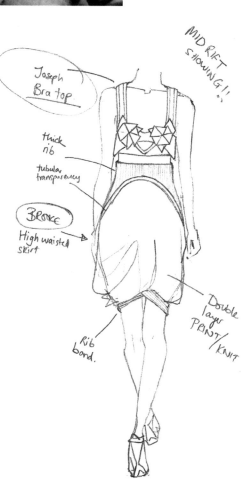

MID RIFT SHOWING!!

Joseph Bra top

thick rib

tubular transparency

BROKE
High waisted skirt

Double layer PRINT/KNIT

Rib bond.

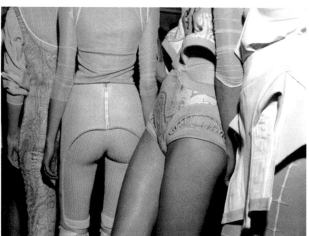

How would you define British fashion? *Confident, innovative, raw, new and stylish.*

What are the pros and cons of working in London for a designer? *I travel between London and Italy. My factory is based in Como, where I make all my fabric developments, prototypes and production. London is where I create the essence of the collection. It is incredibly inspiring and nostalgic to me – I love designing from my studio here. London can equally be depressing, particularly when there are cash-flow restrictions – money always creeps up on you and there are high demands when starting a new label. It can be a real struggle in this city, although creatively, there is such a refined structure and order about London that I find very unique.*

Does working in Britain inform your work? *I feel at home in London. There is a natural ability and comfort for me here; I have a creative energy that just flows. I am a spiritual person and somehow atmospheres really affect my mood and ability. There is something about designing a collection at home that makes me feel alive and inspired.*

Why do you think London has a reputation for creating new design talent? *An individual needs to be prepared to struggle and fight here. A lot of the talent comes from Central St Martins College of Art and Design. Motivation is the keyword. One needs to be motivated and passionate to move forward – there is no textbook rule of how to create a new talent – CSM gives each student the freedom to develop in his/her own way. I think that is why most talent not only comes from London but also comes from CSM.*

Does British fashion history ever inform your work? *British architecture does, it is so visually complex, detailed, structured and very English! I am completely inspired by buildings such as St Paul's and its Whispering Gallery, The Houses of Parliament and Westminster Abbey.*

How do you think British designers and British fashion are regarded internationally? *I think people respect British designers and they are intrigued as to what makes the best designers emerge specifically from here.*

Do you think there is a distinct British style? *No, everyone is accepted for individual style.*

Which other British designers do you admire and why? *I admire Alexander McQueen for building what I highly regard as an established brand with worldwide stores in a relatively short space of time. I admire the fact that McQueen has maintained such creative strength inside of what also needs to be a commercially viable corporation* 🇬🇧

| **p.138** | top left, top right & middle left An indigo blue short-sleeved jumper encrusted with black Swarovski crystals showed the designer's technical advances in A/W 2008; middle right Sketch for S/S 2009, showing the complexity of Goldin's designs; bottom S/S 2009 | **p.139** | S/S 2009 explored the potential for an organic yet heavily constructed version of knitwear

BRITISH ECCENTRICS **FUEL** THE COLLECTIONS OF LUELLA

A self-proclaimed English eccentric, Luella Bartley designs clothes that 'you can get drunk and fall over in'. Epitomizing quirky British style, her collections are based on a philosophy of 'rock meets granny, meets geek, meets Sloane'.

Luella Bartley grew up in Stratford-Upon-Avon before studying fashion journalism at Central St Martins College of Art and Design. She went on to work as a fashion journalist for *The Evening Standard*, *Vogue*, *The Face* and *Dazed & Confused*. In 2000, she decided to refocus her career and launched her own collection called 'Daddy, I want a Pony'.

Since then, Bartley has defined a unique aesthetic that is based on her personal interpretation of Britishness. She frequently references British music history and the Royal Family. 'Tradition is very important,' she explains. 'It's a huge part of what influences me and British culture is steeped in it. I love tradition.'

Believing that her style is contrary, Bartley says, 'I like things that don't mix well – they always end up getting along brilliantly.' During her design process, Bartley always begins with a character – Britt Ekland in *The Wicker Man* (1973) inspired her Autumn/Winter 2008–09 collection and for Spring/Summer 2008 Thora Birch in *Ghost World* (2001) was her muse – which then informs the form and the fabric. Her design icons are also inherently British and include the Duchess of Devonshire, Princess Anne, Agatha Christie, Mary Quant, Paula Yates, Amy Winehouse, Siouxsie Sioux and Vivienne Westwood. 'As long as you are being true to what you like, does it really matter if it's modern? Not for personal style anyway,' states Bartley. 'I think being individual and experimental is modern.'

Bartley's fashion success allowed her to show at New York Fashion Week for six years. 'This was partly for commercial reasons and to reach a bigger audience,' she explains. 'But also partly because New York has that similar cultural undercurrent and inspiring music and art history and is informed by its youth.'

Collaborations have also defined Bartley's work, and have included working with people from Noki to Church's shoes. 'I like to work with like-minded people and sometimes with people that I just can't understand but love and people that I respect and look up to. Each of my favourite collaborations has a very British undertone.' For Spring/Summer 2002, Bartley created her first collection for high-street store New Look. In the same year, she worked with Mulberry to design the Gisele bag, which revived the ailing brand.

In 2007, Bartley returned to show in London, where she also opened a new shop on Brook Street. Her signature prom dresses have become the uniform for young female songstresses from Lily Allen to Kate Nash. 'I thoroughly enjoy seeing the girls getting excited about wearing my clothes,' she enthuses. 'There is nothing more validating than when a customer gets a kick out of something

| **pp.140–141** | Luella's S/S 2008 collection, wearable feminine clothes with a punk edge, was presented in the ballroom of luxury London hotel Claridge's | **p.142** | top Prom dresses are a signature style; sketches 1–3 drawn for A/W 2007; sketches 4–5 for S/S 2008; bottom Luella's A/W 2008 collection was inspired by girly punks and rich kids who have raided their granny's wardrobes | **p.143** | A/W 2008

I design. I do love it when the show comes together and you see the idea become a real person. The character has come full circle and comes alive – the hair, the make-up, the shoes – that is a very exciting and fulfilling moment.'

Essentially British, Bartley's collections are both preppy and punk. Her unique edgy Notting Hill style has captivated the international fashion industry. With a basis in London street style, Bartley's clothes are inherently cool and covetable.

How would you define British fashion? *Creativity through adversity. Britain is a pretty tough place to be. It's like when everyone has to try much harder in recession and it brings out really strong creativity. In Britain, it always seems like a struggle and that's how great things happen. The weather, the expense, the lack of support and the harsh judgment from your contemporaries mean you are always being pushed. It's tough, but that's how the British creative seems to function best; when things are good we go to pot, the hard times seem to be the most creative in British culture – look at punk. We also have such a rich cultural history to draw from, whether that is tradition and the upper classes, rebellion and the working classes or the preoccupations of the middle classes. Class has a lot to do with British culture. Also the fashion scene is closely linked to other creative disciplines – art, music, film – and everybody talks and debates and gets drunk together. It all helps.*

Does working in Britain inform your work? *Always. I am nothing short of obsessed with British culture. Most collections have a very British theme running through them and when it's not specifically British, it's still about a British attitude.*

Why do you think London has a reputation for creating new design talent? *Adversity and probably a bit of arrogance that comes from past success. London designers don't really think about the job they can get at the end, it's more about their own label, we are all little snotty St Martins kids with big ideas, even if, like me, you don't really fit that mould. And it's probably a lot to do with our lack of business acumen. Vanity reigns supreme but I think that is starting to change now.*

How do you think British designers and British fashion are regarded internationally? *Slightly mad, untrustworthy and difficult to control, but exciting and untameable.*

Do you think there is a distinct British style? *Yes, but it's all over the place. You can tell a British person by their complete disregard for the rules. It's not so much a uniform as a unified attitude. Our staples would have to be tweed, calf-length skirts, Chelsea boots, skintight jeans, rock T-shirts, pearls and winkle-pickers* 🇬🇧

| **p.144** | A royal garden party was seen at S/S 2009, where Princess Anne hair styles, oversized hair bows, mini-dresses and cashmere cardigans were presented at the Serpentine Gallery, London | **p.145** | top left S/S 2009; top middle & right For A/W 2007, Luella gave a nod to her British roots as she dressed models in red hunting coats and jodhpur-style trousers; bottom Pastel patent trench coats from A/W 2006

MATTHEW WILLIAMSON **LOVES** KALEIDOSCOPIC COLOUR

As a child, Matthew Williamson always envisaged owning a shop with a pink sign over the door. Now, his clothes are synonymous with bright kaleidoscopic colours, vibrant patterns and prints. Often exploring a hippy aesthetic, he designs technicolour garments that celebrate colour in fashion.

Born in Manchester, Matthew Williamson studied fashion at Central St Martins College of Art and Design in London. Graduating in 1994, he worked on a freelance basis with Marni, before being employed by British fashion company Monsoon and Accessorize.

Williamson launched his debut catwalk show in 1997, entitled 'Electric Angels'. The collection was modelled by Jade Jagger, Kate Moss, Helena Christensen and Diane Kruger, and made the front pages of the national newspapers. Bias-cut dresses and separates in bright shades of tangerine, fuchsia and magenta were unique for the time and established Matthew Williamson's signature style.

After several years showing his collection successfully in London, Williamson made the decision to show at New York Fashion Week in 2002. 'The move fundamentally changed perceptions of me within the fashion world,' he explains. 'It made the brand global and I was proud of that achievement. New York is a dynamic city and provides us with the opportunity to show more people what we do.'

In 2004, the first flagship store opened in Mayfair, London, complete with a pink sign above the door. Williamson won ELLE Best British Designer of the Year in 2004, and was awarded the 2005 Moët & Chandon Fashion Tribute. He has also been nominated three times for Designer of the Year at the British Fashion Awards.

| p.146 | Leopard-print dress for A/W 2008
| p.148 | both A/W 2009 | p.149 | top three A/W 2009; bottom S/S 2008

Williamson was appointed creative director of Emilio Pucci, the luxury Italian fashion house, owned by LVMH in 2005. 'Pucci has always been for me the archetypal figure of the elegant aristocrat who embodied Italian design. He intuitively understood the relationship between dynamic shapes and kinetic motifs, and captured the zeitgeist of the modernist interwar period in his collections,' explains Williamson. 'Since being creative director of Emilio Pucci, I have sought to retain these defining brand characteristics, most importantly the infamous prints and the body-conscious silhouette.'

A very special year, 2007 marked the ten-year anniversary of the Matthew Williamson label. The Design Museum in London mounted an exhibition focusing on the design process of his work, and he also celebrated by putting on a one-off show at London Fashion Week.

'I would say that my personal style ultimately remains the same from season to season,' says Williamson. 'Instead, I update my look with elements of current trends through accessories.' Fashion, according to Williamson, works best when it is aspirational and visually exciting. 'I have found that my love of brightly coloured bold prints has helped me to achieve this. Prints have defined

the heritage of the brand and they are very important to me on a personal level.'

Travel and exploration of new countries are key inspirations for Williamson. 'I prefer places that have hot exotic cultures. I always take a camera and sketchbook with me as I love to capture images and memories from trips.' As a consequence, the themes of travel and nature have always been prevalent in Williamson's work.

Seeing people wear his designs with panache allows Williamson to thrive in his work. 'The Matthew Williamson girl likes to wear luxurious dresses full of colour and beautiful details because it is an extension of her fun-loving spirit and glamour.'

Recognized for his sun-drenched prints and dresses, Matthew Williamson has carved himself a niche in the fashion industry. Injecting colour into high fashion, Williamson revels in the exuberance of dressing up.

How would you define British fashion? *British fashion has always been eclectic with a cutting edge. There is a youthfulness found in it, which emerges from street culture. Likewise, the music and art scenes have always had a huge influence on our style.*

Does working in Britain inform your work? *Growing up in Manchester, I perceived my environment as quite grey. Grey skies, grey streets and grey buildings. I felt the need to seek the polar opposite of this in my work. My first collection ('Electric Angels' in 1997) was a blast of colour in a time when the trend was for minimalist, utilitarian almost bland clothing, and this helped to set me apart. I am still very much known for my use of colour and print.*

How do you think British designers and British fashion are regarded internationally? *Over the past few years London Fashion Week has become known as THE place to go to see new talent, and people are not disappointed. There is a hotbed of talent showing here at the moment and the influx of international buyers and press is testament to that.*

Do you think there is a distinct British style? *British style has always been quirky. We have never been afraid to experiment with our clothing as a way of expressing ourselves. We have always had a tradition of impeccable tailoring that is distinct to our style, which flows from Savile Row right down to our high street* ✁✁

| **p.150** | top A/W 2008; middle left Characteristically bright fruit punch colours from S/S 2009; middle right S/S 2002; bottom left Design moodboards for A/W 2008, showing Williamson's influences of pattern, colour and print; bottom right An iconic image from the debut collection, S/S 1998 | **p.151** | Design moodboards for S/S 2009

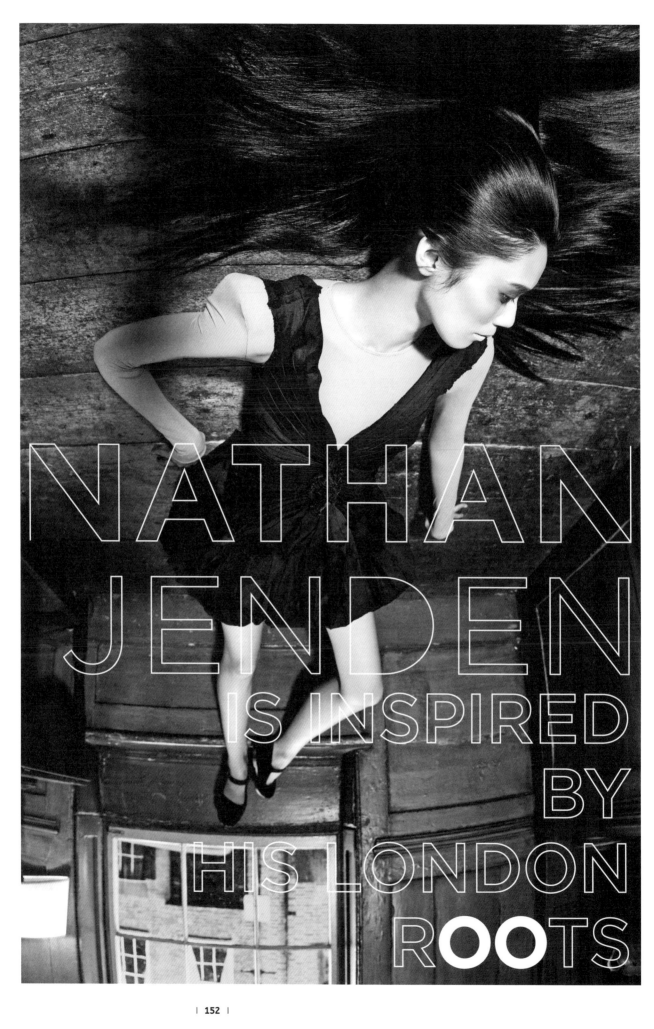

NATHAN JENDEN IS INSPIRED BY HIS LONDON ROOTS

| p.152 | 'Gnoix' dress, A/W 2007 | p.153 |
'Procopia' dress, A/W 2007 | p.154 | all images
& sketches from Jenden's S/S 2009 collection was
a riot of colour as multi-coloured dresses
conveyed a vibrant mood | p.155 | all images
'The Secret History' collection, A/W 2008, which
included high necks and ruffled collars fanned
into pleats on sharp tailored jackets and
dresses with extravagant bows

'A garment is never complete: it can always be better, depending on who's wearing it.' Nathan Jenden's 'perfection is boring' philosophy creates clothes that push the boundaries of taste and wearability thanks to his innovative approach to fabric use and form.

London-born Nathan Jenden studied fashion design at Central St Martins College of Art and Design before undertaking an MA at the Royal College of Art. His strong aesthetic quickly landed him with a job as a designer at Kenzo, after which Jenden went on to assist John Galliano in Paris.

Jenden's ambition and success led him to New York in 1998, where he designed Daryl K's men's and women's collections and was responsible for turning the brand in to a hugely coveted and commercially successful enterprise. After his prestigious position at Daryl K, Jenden moved to design for maverick wrap-dress designer Diane von Furstenberg. In 2001, he was appointed as creative director, working with von Furstenberg to develop the brand in to an internationally influential fashion business.

In 2006, Jenden decided to present his personal design vision and launched his own label with a runway show at Lady Mendl's Tea Salon during New York Fashion Week. His first collection, called 'Angel Heart,' was inspired by 'the drama of a Goya silhouette.' Jenden created tailored ruffled garments that showed a distinct design aesthetic and forward-thinking approach to modern clothing.

Jenden's design philosophy is based on providing collections that fill the gap between the artisan and the factory. 'My designs are tailored and modern,' he explains. 'The clothes are very constructed but have a lightness and modernity. They have a life of their own. They can fit in your wardrobe and that's how people dress now.' Jenden uses craftsmen and women to hand-finish garments that are durable and lasting, as he wants his clothes to portray a beautiful quality.

'Chaotic but determined' is how Jenden describes his design process. 'As soon as you did your best you know you could do better.' Fuelled by the prospect of captivating people, he explains, 'When people enjoy your clothes and are inspired by them, you feel like it is worth trying to say something.'

In 2008, Jenden further enhanced the appeal of his label by unveiling his first-ever eyewear collection on the catwalk. The sought-after pieces were very well received by the fashion press and confirmed Jenden's position as an innovative and directional British designer.

How would you define British fashion? *Irreverent and original.*

What are the pros and cons of working in London for a designer?
It's difficult to really build a business out of London. On the other hand, due to the lack of emphasis on commerciality you have creative freedom.

Why do you think London has a reputation for creating new design talent? *I think that a strong element of this is due to Central St Martins College of Art and Design, and I think that London and the UK have always had a reputation for creating new and different talent in all design disciplines from architecture to film, from graphics to magazines. I think to be a Londoner is to be the very definition of the word 'fusion'. I mainly live in New York, and London is much more of a melting pot.*

Does British fashion history ever inform your work? *Sometimes, but I wouldn't particularly put the emphasis on Britain. British fashion icons inform my work more, such as Elizabeth I and Quentin Crisp.*

How do you think British designers and British fashion are regarded internationally? *Original, creative, a little bit mad and witty.*

Do you think there is a distinct British style? *I think that what is distinct about British style is that it is always important to look like you didn't try too hard. I think it horrifies the British sensibility!*

Which other British designers do you admire and why? *Paul Smith for his business sense and John Galliano for his ability to create emotion in fashion.*

What reference points do you often revisit? *British art from Holbein to Hockney to Hirst* 🇬🇧

| **p.156** | Design sketches for S/S 2008
| **p.157** | Entitled 'Gatecrasher', Jenden's A/W 2007 collection included this spearmint puffball dress

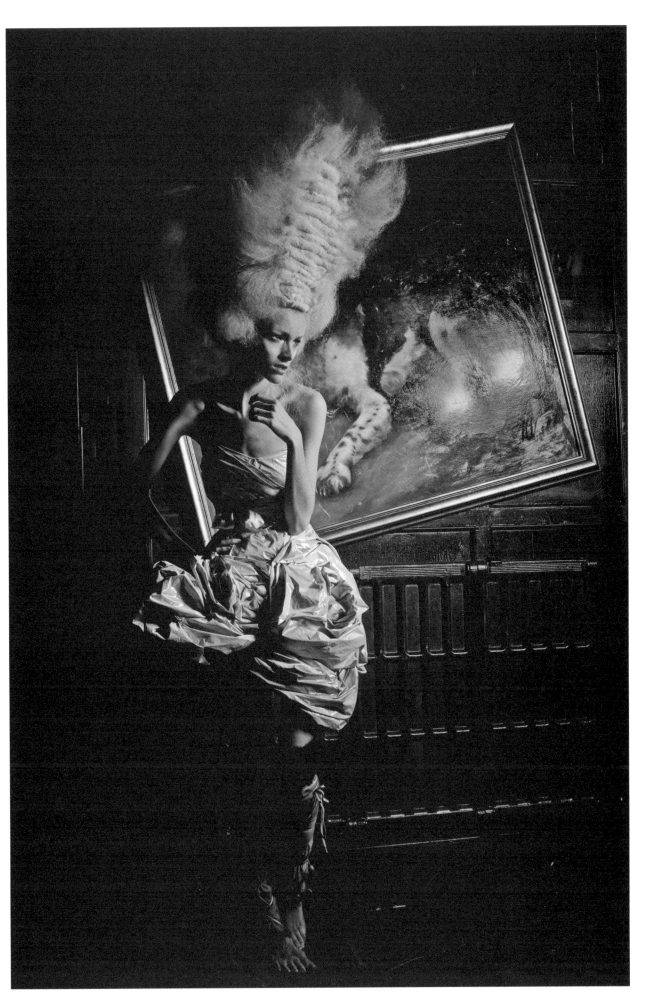

A SUBVERSIVE DESIGNER + CUSTOMIZER, NOKI QUESTIONS FASHION

Noki is an anagram and pun on 'ikon'. Renowned for being a subversive designer, Jonathan 'JJ' Hudson promotes customization as a swipe at the homogeneity of globalized mass-produced fashion.

The Noki label was first created in 1996, when Aberdeen-born Hudson was working as a stylist for MTV. After graduating from Edinburgh College of Art, Hudson became inspired by the idea of creating one-off art products in a move that was focused on 'customizing corporateness.'

Dubbed the 'King of Customization,' Hudson spent ten years successfully fashioning recycled clothing and second-hand fabrics into his own unique brand of street couture. Shunning the limelight, Hudson never shows his face to an audience, always wearing a surgical mask to hide himself from photographers. His garments have been displayed at the Victoria & Albert Museum in London and also at the Metropolitan Museum of Art in New York.

The concept behind Noki owes much to Kalle Lasn, the writer and founder of anti-consumerist magazine *Adbusters*, whom Hudson cites as having a major influence on his work. 'Customization is always a work in progress,' he explains. 'Every garment is always under construction – worn and waiting to be discarded and demanding reinvention.'

In 2007, Noki's work was given a greater focus with the fashion world's interest in eco-friendly clothing. His concept, the Noki House of Sustainability (NHS for short), was a tongue-in-cheek proposition with serious intentions, aiming to reuse clothing. According to Hudson, the Noki style is a slow burner: 'It has no male or female barriers, even sizing in the garments is removed, everyone is encouraged to fulfill a fantasy and try it on, setting sustainability free.'

Hudson's contribution to fashion proves that the designer has not bowed to accepted Western design ideas of creating luxurious new garments. By taking the idea of sustainability to new heights and by challenging what is considered high fashion, Hudson has questioned the current aesthetic and established ideals in contemporary fashion design. With a nod to punk, Noki represents the British attitude of rebellion and new ideas.

How would you define British fashion? *British fashion is a reaction to the isolation of living on an island and is based on a need to create change from within a relatively small population.*

What are the pros and cons of working in London for a designer? *London is a very unique place where its history demands and creates the best thinking there is. It's a diverse melting pot that produces levels of acceptance like no other great city. London will accept, love and nurture true thinking if its time is right. This is not a given if London's infrastructure is not ready to listen – it can*

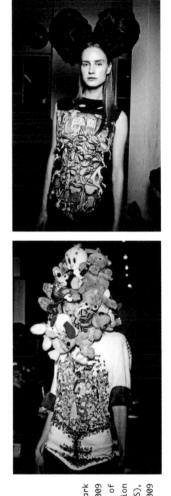

| **p.158** | Shot during the making of Mark Lebon's fashion film 'Dr Noki NHS', A/W 2009 | **p.160** | Piers Atkinson created all sorts of weird and wonderful hats for his collaboration with the Noki House of Sustainability (NHS), A/W 2009 | **p.161** | all images A/W 2009

also ignore, isolate and destroy a spirit that demands too much attention. To be creative in London sharpens the senses and brings forth futuristic visions.

Does working in Britain inform your work? *All information and the homogenization of that information spread through a relatively small population in Britain is what informs and sharpens Noki's senses for change.*

Why do you think London has a reputation for creating new design talent? *Britain as a whole is a tiny island in the grand scale of other world cultures. We, as a small nation, are pretty well in tune with what our fellow Brits are thinking and, in a fashion world, are wearing. This creates a stand-off to homogenization and it is here where our design talents find their special niche. They bring forth new ideas to break down this harmful barrier against creativity.*

Does British fashion history ever inform your work? *Any fashion history brings up questions of what made them do it – the 'why' factor – be it political, economic or just pure demand for 'environmental' change. It is these factors I look at in parallel to make sense of why these special style statements and silhouettes evolve to become our fashion history.*

How do you think British designers and British fashion are regarded internationally? *Our industry is looked upon like the serious clowns, the cultural entertainment. Other nations that have industrial and government support get inspired by our outrageous demand for change and re-appropriate it into a more acceptable silhouette. It is this sense of isolation that stops any complacent attitude to why our visions are the way they are. There is no compromise, a 'talent' window of opportunity to shine is only small, hence the extremity of the creativity.*

Do you think there is a distinct British style? *True British style is traditionally dandy and moves and shakes to an extreme measure at the best of times. It breaks down traditions and always keeps an eye on its position within acceptability without alienation. It's as though British style is a desire to attract the free thinkers away from the crowd, to re-establish a truth and clarity.*

Which other British designers do you admire and why? *I admire all my fellow 'artists' because they have survived the first flourish of their initial ideas. They have gotten over their hardest hurdle; to be taken seriously in any industry in Britain is a huge achievement. And, 'why', because you are inspiring fellow Brits to keep the pattern of this creativity going* 🇬🇧

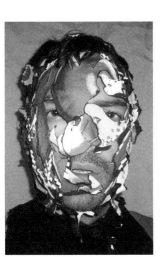

| **p.162** | top four images For his S/S 2008 collection, Noki introduced the concept of NOKI-NHS-Customisation and Aftercare Service (NHS standing for 'Noki House of Sustainability'); bottom left Skin from Skunk Anansie models for Noki's A/W 2009 collection; middle 'The Pen Work Tears of a Clown' artwork for A/W 2008; bottom right Photographed from inside a mask, A/W 2008 | **p.163** | Noki is famous for hiding behind masks: 'The Suffocation of Branding', A/W 2008

QUIRKY BRITISH **STYLE** IS THE HANDWRITING OF PAUL SMITH

'I give classics just a little kick,' notes one of the most commercially successful British designers, Sir Paul Smith, who sells a distinctive British lifestyle to consumers around the world.

Without any formal qualifications and with early ambitions of becoming a professional cyclist dashed after an accident, Paul Smith focused on a different passion: clothes. He opened his first store in Nottingham in 1970, and has since worked to define the now globally recognized Paul Smith aesthetic.

Within 20 years of setting up his label, Smith had established himself as a pre-eminent British designer. With an ability to combine a sense of humour and mischief with a love of tradition and the classics, Smith has retained his core value of creating quality well-made clothes. 'I suppose that a lot of my work is based on tradition,' he explains, 'reusing traditional fabrics in a new way or traditional methods of manufacturing but always giving them a new twist.'

Smith describes himself as 'a curious mind mixing the past and the present, the kitsch and the beautiful, but always with a sense of humour.' He showed his first menswear collection in Paris in 1976, and his company is now a huge global brand, selling clothes in over 35 countries and from 14 shops within the UK alone.

'I design clothes that are for the wearer to enjoy rather than what I call attention-seeking clothes.' This means simple classical shapes often with quirky details, such as different coloured buttons, interesting lining and unusual fabrics. 'My clothes have elements of craftsmanship, classicism and tradition, but are always designed with a contemporary aspect.'

Benefiting from a loyal customer base, the Paul Smith brand has grown to appeal to a wide selection of individuals. Michael Hamilton from Belfast's menswear store Bureau subscribes to Paul Smith's vision. 'We have customers who only want to buy "Smithy." They have been wearing Paul Smith from when they got their first grant or pay cheque and 19 years later they are still buying it.' Hamilton believes it is Smith's signature style that maintains customer loyalty. 'There is a certain sense of seriousness but with two fingers to convention. His clothes can be quite beautiful and serious but still have those little touches of subtle details that bring a smile to the wearer's face.' Customers trust the Paul Smith brand as it has always communicated the importance of quality. One of the things that separates Paul Smith from many of the other established 'safe' brands is his faithfulness to good well-executed design; his collections are design led.

In 1995, the London-based Design Museum opened a Paul Smith retrospective, looking at his work in the fashion business over a 25-year period. Called 'True Brit', the exhibition marked the first time this renowned museum had devoted an entire show to a single

| **pp.164–165** | Tailoring is the key to Paul Smith – this coat and floral pattern shirt from his A/W 2008 menswear collection demonstrate Smith's ability to produce wearable and practical garments

| **p.166** | top left & bottom middle S/S 2008; middle left Smith promised 'a hint of Sixties, a taste of Bohemian and a few classics' for his Women Black collection, A/W 2005; top middle S/S 2007; top right Women Black A/W 2007; bottom left & right Women Black collection, A/W 2008
| **p.167** | Classic shirts with a twist from S/S 2008

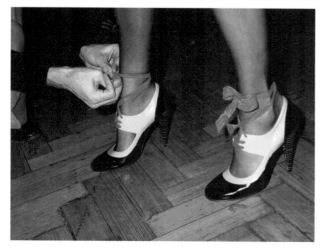

| **p.168** | top Men's A/W 2007; middle & bottom Tailored coats and shoes from Women's A/W 2007 collection | **p.169** | top Vibrant colour is a Paul Smith signature, shown here in A/W 2007; middle Men's A/W 2008; bottom left & right The S/S 2007 collection communicates his quirky but casual approach to menswear

fashion designer, thereby underlining the importance of Smith's contribution to international fashion.

Globally, there are 12 different collections produced under the Paul Smith name, which include womenswear, childrenswear, watches, furniture, rugs, china, spectacles and fragrances. Designed in Nottingham and London, the Paul Smith collections are mainly produced in England and Italy, while the fabrics used tend to be of Italian, French and British origin.

In 2002, Smith collaborated with Cappellini to create a furniture collection called 'Mondo,' inspired by Smith's observation and travel. In 2003, he designed an upholstery textile, called 'Bespoke' and inspired by classic pinstripe suiting, in partnership with famous textiles company Maharam. 'Most of my design icons are architects or product designers,' explains Smith, whose foray into the decorative arts has been an influential aspect of his business.

Paul Smith continues to be an integral part of the company; he is both designer and chairman. As he wrote in his book, *You Can Find Inspiration in Everything*, 'The reason I've been successful is because I've just got on and packed boxes and I know that VAT means Value Added Tax not vodka and tonic. I've sold on the shop floor, I've typed invoices. At some point, I've done everything, and I've always kept my head above water financially. Nevertheless, I'm extremely nervous about becoming a businessman and not a designer.'

Smith puts his success down to 'lateral thinking, to not going down the obvious route and to mixing things in a way that is not expected.' Although he is an internationally celebrated fashion artist, Smith remains very much down to earth. He frequently visits his shops, talks to customers and learns about his clientele's needs.

A key component of the British fashion industry, Paul Smith offers British clothing with a twist. By combining garments in an unusual manner or by using striking colours to make modern and progressive pieces, Smith has built a hugely successful business on a distinct Anglo aesthetic. With reference to the tradition of British tailoring, Smith's clothing has international appeal and relevance ✂✂

| **p.170** | Jeans collection, A/W 2008 | **p.171** | top left Women Black, A/W 2007; top right A quintessentially British look from A/W 2008; middle left Women Black, S/S 2008; middle centre Fresh lady-like chic from Women Black, S/S 2007; middle right S/S 2006; bottom left & right The Jeans collection for men is a more affordable and younger range, A/W 2008

THE **HAT**S OF PHILIP TREACY ARE THE WORK OF A **MASTER** CRAFTSMAN

'I am constantly challenging the perception of what a hat should be and what role it should play,' explains master milliner Philip Treacy. 'I think and hope I have challenged the way we look at hats. They are no longer symbols of conformity but highly individual acts of rebellion.'

Born in 1966 in the West of Ireland, Philip Treacy moved to Dublin in 1985 to study fashion at the National College of Art and Design, where he started making hats 'as a hobby.' When students undertook work experience, Treacy spent six weeks with London-based hat designer Stephen Jones.

Going on to study at the Royal College of Art in London, Treacy focused on his love of hat design. 'It was at a time when hats were perceived publicly as something worn by ladies of a certain age, and something from a bygone era,' says Treacy. 'I thought this was totally ridiculous and simply believed we all have a head, so everybody has the possibility of wearing a hat.'

In 1989, Treacy took one of his hats to Michael Roberts, then fashion director of *Tatler* magazine, and his style editor, Isabella Blow. Blow was so impressed she asked Treacy to make a hat for her wedding. She became Treacy's patron and he worked from the basement of her house in Belgravia, London. Since, Treacy has not only created his own collection but has also collaborated with many designers, including Ralph Lauren, Donna Karan, Alexander McQueen, Rifat Ozbek, Gianni Versace and Valentino.

'A hat is a positive symbol,' explains Treacy. 'A good hat is the ultimate glamour accessory. It thrills observers and makes the wearer feel a million dollars.' Treacy's hats are very desirable, and his message is simple: a great hat exists outside its own time.

By 1991, Treacy was designing hats for Chanel, the first of which was a twisted birdcage, photographed by Patrick Demarchelier and worn by Linda Evangelista on the cover of British *Vogue*. In the same year and also in 1992, the British Fashion Council named Treacy British Accessory Designer of the Year.

A defining moment in his career, his first fashion show of all black hats was staged in 1993. The supermodels of the time – Naomi Campbell, Yasmin Le Bon, Kate Moss, Stella Tennant and Christy Turlington – all modeled for him.

In 1994, Treacy opened a shop in London and his hats have also been exhibited at the Victoria & Albert Museum, the Hayward Gallery and the Crafts Council in London and at the Powerhouse Museum in Sydney. In 2000, Treacy was invited by the Chambre Syndicale de la Haute Couture to present the first ever haute couture show in Paris devoted to hats. As a result of his contribution to the British fashion industry, Treacy was awarded an OBE by HRH Prince Charles and HRH The Duchess of Cornwall in 2007.

| **p.172** | The 'Hand Hat', 2006, is a nod to Surrealism, a theme which Treacy often explores | **p.174** | top 'Madonna Rides Again', 2001; bottom this hat from 2001 illustrates how the designer challenges traditional shapes of headwear | **p.175** | Sketch (by fashion illustrator David Downton) and image of the 'Red Comet Hat', 2001, a dynamic statement piece that defines Treacy's innovative approach to hat design

The hats begin their life as drawings. They are then mocked up in a light flexible fabric, called sparterie, and sent to Treacy's block maker in Paris who carves the actual shape in wood. 'I depend on his desire and skill to make his block look exactly like the form I give him and to capture every single nuance of the original shape because in hat-making, even a fraction of an inch is crucial. It's all very precise.'

Thriving on producing work that is relevant today, Treacy explains, 'People always ask me if I would have preferred to live in a more "hat" era, such as the 1920s or 1940s, but I think it is much more exciting to work today. I use contemporary influences, be it sculpture or art or whatever is going on in the world today. We live in the present and we should be making contemporary hats and showing them in a different and new way.'

How would you define British fashion? *Fashion is not known for its humanity. It's about everything but that; fashion people are very unusual, they are obsessed with perfection and life isn't like that. I think that is what my Irishness does for me; it gives me humanity. There is no such thing as playtime when you work in fashion, because it is all encompassing.*

Does working in Britain inform your work? *Hats are part of English dress and culture: weddings, Ascot, Henley, etc. But we have an international audience who are seduced by glamour, and glamour is and always will be attractive to men and women. So glamour is a good currency to work in and there is nothing more glamorous than a hat.*

Why do you think London has a reputation for creating new design talent? *London has the best of everything life has to offer. To quote Samuel Johnson, 'When a man is tired of London, he is tired of life.'*

Does British fashion history ever inform your work? *Hat-making has been around since the beginning of time; it's part of every culture. I haven't invented the hat; I have just sort of made it sexy. One of the most exciting aspects of my job is that I have an opportunity to influence how people see hats in the twenty-first century. And that is a very exciting job, because I have a worldwide audience open to seeing hats in a new way.*

Which other British designers do you admire and why? *I am not trying to be diplomatic, but I've worked with so many that I really can't choose. It's exciting to work with strong designers, such as Alexander McQueen, because they let you interpret their style. Some designers are specific, but many designers that I have worked with for a long time give me free rein to design with their collections in mind* 🇬🇧

p.176 | top left The 'White Feather Fountain' hat, 2001; top right Treacy's hats are often humorous and poke fun at the idea of wearing a hat, as seen here with 'Hat' hat, 2001; middle three images White structured wave hat, a silver disk hat and a natural button hat with rose and hand-cut feather, all from S/S 2009; bottom left White sinamay bow, S/S 2009; bottom right Snake sinamay structure wave hat, S/S 2009 | **p.177** | both Drawings by Treacy for his 2008 collection

ROCK'**N**'ROLL-INSPIRED + DE-CONSTRUCTED CLOTHING IS THE TRADEMARK OF PREEN

'We are organic and work very naturally on feelings and thoughts,' state London-based designers Justin Thornton and Thea Bregazzi. 'There is no real philosophy.'

Preen is Justin Thornton and Thea Bregazzi. Both come from The Isle of Man where they first met at the age of 18 on an art foundation course. Thornton graduated from Winchester School of Art and went on to design the successful 'Second Life' collection for designer Helen Storey; Bregazzi began work as a freelance designer after graduating from the University of Central Lancashire. The pair first worked together when Helen Storey asked them to advise on her Autumn/Winter 1996–97 collection.

Inspired by the experience of designing together, they launched Preen in 1996. 'Every day is like a collaboration between us,' explain the designers, who describe their design process as 'natural, experimental, technical and fun'. Sold from their boutique in Portobello Road, London, the first Preen collection comprised one-off pieces and were an immediate hit with fashion stylists and celebrities.

Building on their early success, Bregazzi and Thornton have seen an increase in sales and extensive press attention with subsequent collections. They have earned a reputation as one of London's most skilled design teams for their imaginative takes on traditional forms. Their original look was described as a 'distinctive modern Victoriana look', as they took inspiration from the early Britons, the Victorian era and punk trash.

Deconstruction and reconstruction of garments is a key theme in Preen's work. 'We often revisit the classics like a man's dress shirt, the trench or suit pants,' they say. Signature materials include natural classic fabrics like silk, cashmere, wool and linen, battered leather, lace, tulle, glazed cotton, old jewelry and buttons.

In the spring of 2001, Preen debuted at London Fashion Week. In 2003, they launched a menswear line and began showing their collections in New York in 2007 to reach a wider commercial audience. Preen now presents two catwalk collections a year in two different capitals and has two lines: 'Preen by Thornton and Bregazzi' and 'Preen Line'.

How would you define British fashion? *Directional, haphazard, classic, fusion.*

What are the pros and cons of working in London for a designer? *It's a creative, experimental, multicultural and inspiring city with so much history and lots of new ideas.*

Does British fashion history ever inform your work? *Yes, in costume and traditional crafts* ⽻

| **p.179** | A/W 2003 | **p.180** | top left A/W 2006; all other images A/W 2004, an edgy and attitude-heavy collection featuring cleverly folded sheepskin flying jackets, high collars and signature draped jersey dresses | **p.181** | Beautiful back detailing for S/S 2009

| **p.182** | S/S 2007 | **p.183** | top left A/W 2009;
top right Vibrant colour for A/W 2006; bottom
three images Preen Line S/S 2009

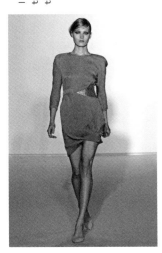

A SLOUCHY SIGNATURE STYLE HAS BEEN **CREATE**D BY STELLA McCARTNEY

'Naturally sexy, naturally confident and modern,' is how Stella McCartney describes her fashion aesthetic. She mixes effortless-ness with sex appeal and fuses seduction and sport. With strong anti-fur beliefs, McCartney has a poignant vision that is increasingly relevant within the modern fashion industry.

Born in London, Stella McCartney, daughter of iconic musician Sir Paul McCartney, studied at Central St Martins College of Art and Design. During her time at college, she undertook work placements at Christian Lacroix and also with a tailor on Savile Row, which, she explains, 'had an everlasting impact on my work.'

In 1995, McCartney graduated and her much-hyped degree collection was worn by her friends, the supermodels Naomi Campbell and Kate Moss. The collection established her signature style of fusing tailored garments with feminine pieces inspired by lingerie.

McCartney immediately set up her own-name label and after two successful collections, she was appointed as creative director of Chloé in Paris in 1997. In 2001, she left her position at Chloé to launch her own fashion house under her name, in a joint venture with the Gucci Group. The brand includes luxury ready-to-wear, shoes, bags, fragrances, eyewear, accessories and an organic skin-care range.

'You have to feel comfortable in the clothes,' explains McCartney. 'I think that you have to wear clothes that work for you and that make sense on the person.' As a vegetarian, she refuses to use any leather or fur in her designs and is keen to promote ethical fashion.

Various stimuli inspire McCartney: 'I think it really depends. I nor-mally take my reference points from current points and try and pick up on what's going on around the world now. I look back on periods like the 1970s, 1980s and 1990s. It really depends on the collection as sometimes I can be inspired by the city.'

Knowing when a garment is complete is paramount to McCartney. 'It just clicks, it just works,' she states. 'You know you can just feel it, you can see it in the fit, sometimes it takes a second, sometimes it can take months.' And, the reward for this intense process is when customers feel drawn to her clothes: 'Seeing women wearing the clothes is the most important thing.'

McCartney has collaborated with several artists, including Gary Hume in 2002, David Remfry in 2002 and Robert Crumb in 2005. She worked with Jeff Koons on her Spring/Summer 2006 collection, using his prints on dresses and accessories. 'It's a great opportunity to think outside the box and to try and expand outside the brand,' says McCartney. 'Collaborations enable you to get a chance to work with incredibly talented people. It takes you out of your own working environment into someone else's, which can sometimes be valuable and re-energize what you do.'

| **p.184** | Black and white stripes adorn the hem of a striking dress for A/W 2006 | **p.186** | Adidas collaboration, S/S 2009 | **p.187** | top & middle Adidas collaboration, S/S 2009; bottom three images Dusky shades for A/W 2009

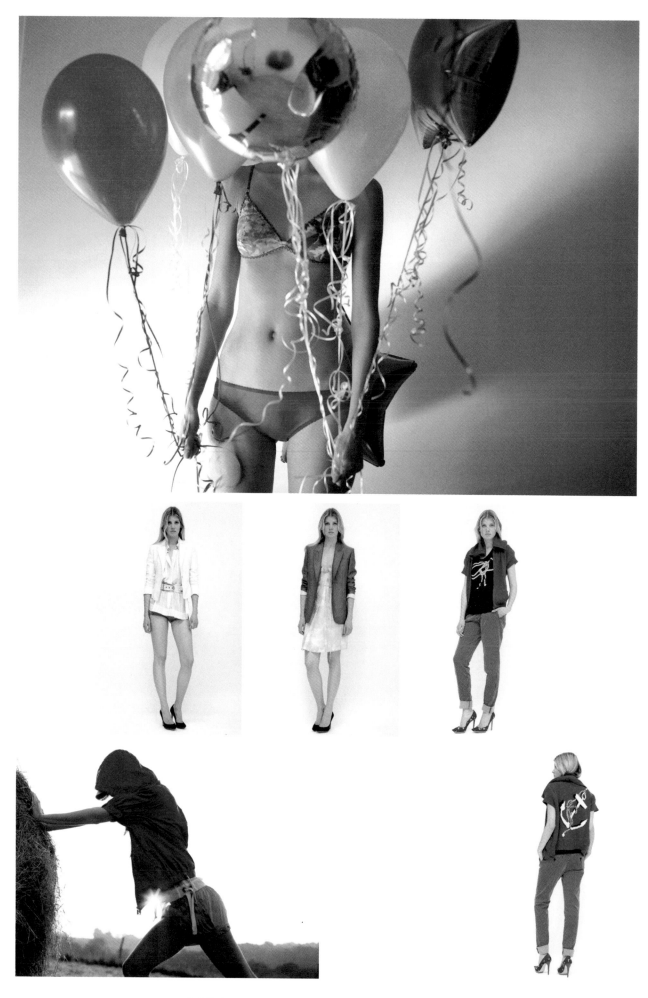

In 2004, McCartney launched a sports performance range with Adidas, offering specific garments for running, gym, yoga, tennis, swimming, dance, golf and winter sports. In 2005, the 'Stella McCartney for H&M' collection sold out worldwide and brought the Stella McCartney look to a different audience.

How would you define British fashion? *I think British fashion is not afraid to have a voice, being the home of punk; this reflects strongly on British fashion and design. It can be very understated and chic, but also very eclectic and eccentric at the same time. I think British fashion understands the different cultures of fashion and tries to relate it in its own voice.*

| **p.188** | Along with extending the brand to include lingerie, the Adidas collection has been a hugely successful collaboration that introduced sportswear into a fashion-focused arena, all S/S 2009 | **p.189** | monochrome shades and shoulder-pads on the catwalk, S/S 2009

What are the pros and cons of working in London for a designer? *The benefits are you can attract a great design team because people want to live in London. I think a lot of people who work in the fashion industry are from London so they sometimes want to come home. The benefits are that it's an incredibly inspiring city, everything comes to London – every gig, every exhibition, every theatrical performance. You get to see the world in London. It's one of the greatest cities in the world, full of artists and young designers and great musicians.*

Why do you think London has a reputation for creating new design talent? *By having one of the best fashion colleges in the world – Central St Martins breeds fantastic new talent.*

Does British fashion history ever inform your work? *I just think that fashion history in general informs my work but I tend to try and look to the future actually and take a bit of inspiration from both.*

How do you think British designers and British fashion are regarded internationally? *We are regarded as some of the best designers in the world. I think we are up there with the best.*

Do you think there is a distinct British style? *British people are not afraid to have a voice and to present an individual language when they dress. Designers do not dictate to them and they always put together their own looks that they are confident in. This is evident in how they look, they have a great spirit of humour. British people always have an irreverent side to them, which is slightly cocky and punk.*

Which other British designers do you admire and why? *I admire every designer as it's not an easy job. Fashion design is not just about the designers who head up the brand, but also about the team that works with them. I think they should all be admired*

SOME OF **THE MOST** BEAUTIFUL HATS IN THE WORLD ARE CREATED BY STEPHEN JONES

'Stephen Jones is the maker of the most beautiful hats in the world,' affirms Anna Piaggi of Italian *Vogue*. With work steeped in couture and craft, Jones has been producing astounding hats for over 25 years and is regarded as one of the most original milliners.

Born in Cheshire, England, Stephen Jones studied at Central St Martins College of Art and Design in the late 1970s. By 1980, Jones had opened his first millinery store in London's Covent Garden, selling hats to rock stars and royalty, including Boy George and Lady Diana.

Defining his aesthetic as 'chic humour', Jones creates millinery that is modern and exciting. He uses materials that are often radical, and his creations range from being beautiful and refined to whimsical.

Citing Elsa Schiaparelli, Charles James and Santiago Calatrava as his design icons, Jones finds wide and varied inspiration, but admits to revisiting the 1940s, 1976 and music for stimulus. 'Tradition is the anchor,' he explains, as his design process is based on his passion of sketching: 'I never stop drawing.'

Collaborations are integral to Jones's success. 'They are essential. I have a long history of collaboration and in part I invented it.' Jones has worked with such artists as Kylie Minogue and Dita Von Teese, but his truly innovative work has been for the catwalk collections of iconic designers including Rei Kawakubo at Comme des Garçons, Vivienne Westwood, Claude Montana, Thierry Mugler, Jean Paul Gaultier, Marc Jacobs and John Galliano for Dior. He also created the regal headpieces that Cate Blanchett wore in the films *Elizabeth* (1998) and *Elizabeth: The Golden Age* (2007).

Jones's work has been exhibited at the Victoria & Albert Museum in London, the Louvre in Paris, The Fashion Institute of Technology and the Brooklyn Museum in New York, the Kyoto Costume Institute in Japan and the National Gallery of Australia in Canberra.

In addition to his 'Model Millinery' main collection, Jones designs 'Miss Jones' and 'Jones Boy' diffusion ranges and a 'Jones Girl' accessories collection made exclusively for Japan. In 2008, he launched his first fragrance in collaboration with Comme des Garçons Parfum. The packaging – a miniature glossy black hatbox – houses a black bottle, the design of which was based on an old ink bottle Jones found in Paris that dates back to the 1890s.

Jones's hat creations have played an integral part in many memorable runway spectacles over the last 25 years. Regarded as a genius of his craft, Jones presents work that is modern and reflects the current zeitgeist. Producing groundbreaking designs, he continually questions contemporary hat design and pushes the boundaries of the acceptable forward: 'I get bored too quickly to be a perfectionist,' admits Jones, whose dedication to innovation within hat design has greatly influenced contemporary fashion.

| **p.191** | 'Wash'n'Go' from the S/S 1993 collection, as shown in *AnOther* magazine | **p.192** | top left 'Taxi'; A/W 2008; top right one of a set of British stamps featuring Jones's 'Top Hat', 2001; hat made for the model Erin O'Connor, 2006 | **p.193** | 'Honey Hat'; S/S 2008

How would you define British fashion? *Vibrant.*

What are the pros and cons of working in London for a designer?
Independence and visibility.

Does working in Britain inform your work? *Yes, I am part of the
British paradox, the punk gent.*

**Why do you think London has a reputation for creating new
design talent?** *The art colleges and democracy.*

Does British fashion history ever inform your work? *Yes,
especially Hartnell, etc.*

**How do you think British designers and British fashion are
regarded internationally?** *As a design hothouse, but ephemeral.*

Do you think there is a distinct British style? *Yes: formal
but inventive.*

Which other British designers do you admire and why? *Giles
Deacon for his European sense of chic. It's very difficult to do
in the UK* 🇬🇧

| **p.194** | 'Curioser and Curioser' hat, S/S 2005
| **p.195** | top left 'Lupina'; A/W 2006; top right
'Tube Hat'; middle left 'Earlham Street' hat;
middle right 'Larissa'; A/W 2006; bottom left
'Tit Tat Hat'; bottom right Hat for Comme des
Garçons catwalk collection, S/S 2006

VIVIENNE WESTWOOD IS THE **QUEEN** OF BRITISH FASHION

Vivienne Westwood is the quintessential British fashion designer. As a radical, opinionated and uncompromising innovator, Westwood has continually challenged established codes of dress.

Vivienne Westwood needs little introduction. Born in 1941 in Derbyshire, England, she invented the punk movement with her then partner and manager of The Sex Pistols Malcolm McLaren and changed the face of British fashion.

From her and McLaren's shop, World's End, in London's Chelsea, Westwood shaped her original ideas, and she continues to drive British fashion to this day. As the benchmark for innovative fashion design, Westwood's iconic style and fashion ideas have placed her at the forefront of contemporary fashion.

Westwood's visionary concepts and clothes have always been against the grain of mainstream fashion. As an individual, she is considered avant-garde, challenging and one of a kind. She is lauded as one of the most important and creative British designers; from punk to pirates and new romantics, Westwood has created exceptional periods in British fashion and has advanced the industry in unrivaled ways. Westwood's contribution to British fashion is unparalleled.

Do you have a design philosophy? *My clothes are uncompromising and allow you to project your personality through them. They are quite theatrical in the sense that they are real clothes, well designed, but they give you a chance to express yourself. They are also inviting – people respond to them and want to come and talk to you.*

How would you describe your clothes? *If everybody is wearing the same thing, they are all bound to look the same. The majority of people on the street look quite dreadful, as they would prefer to say nothing through their clothes than make a mistake. They are lazy in their dress and take no time to express themselves. My clothes, on the other hand, allow someone to be truly individual.*

What do your clothes offer the wearer? *What I think my clothes give people is the power to make them feel sexy – after all they are very feminine. But what is even more important is that they talk about the body in a way that makes you stand out. There is a form to it all, a relation between you and what you are wearing that is terribly interesting; you are doing something that you have never seen done before, and nobody else is wearing anything quite like it. What I think they can do for you is to make you look and feel important. They give you clout.*

How are you modern within fashion? *The last thing I am interested in is keeping up with the times. People are so busy keeping up with the times that they miss everything that is in front of them. I look at paintings, clothes in museums and photographs of couture. If you can grasp what is original about design, you can use it.*

| **p.196** | Signature dramatic and voluminous gowns for the A/W 2006 Vivienne Westwood collection | **p.198** | top Floral shirt from Westwood's 'Anglomania' collection, S/S 2009; bottom 'MAN' collection, S/S 2009, inspired by groups of Romani Gypsy men

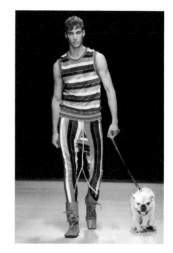

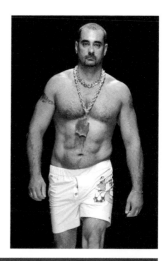

| p.199 | top left Model's headband shows Westwood's support of the Active Resistance to Propaganda manifesto, 'Anglomania', S/S 2009; top right 'MAN', S/S 2009; middle both 'Do It Yourself', S/S 2009; bottom Sketches for 'Gold', (left) and 'African' (right) collections, S/S 2009

| **p.200** | top left An iconic image from S/S 1994, showing dramatic, voluminous dresses with historical references; top right Tailored suits in bespoke tartan first hit the catwalks in 1993 and still inspire more recent collections, as seen here in A/W 2008; bottom left Sketch for 'Gold' collection, S/S 2009; bottom right both 'Anglomania'; A/W 2008 | **p.201** | both images 'MAN'; S/S 2009

How would you describe your design process? *There are all kinds of things you notice and realize that you can translate into something new. Usually, you don't see the source of my translation. It has been transformed into something else by the time I present it. I think the real powerhouse of why you want to continue is that you want to continually surprise yourself. My clothes get freer, the more and more I continue. The technique becomes so automatic.*

What informs your ideas? *A large influence on the collection is the fabric that I use. I use mainly natural fabrics – English barathea, Scottish tartan, Harris and Donegal tweed, English mohair and Swiss silk. I am also influenced by my interest in new pattern-cutting techniques.*

What is the most rewarding part of what you do? *I'm a fashion designer. The greatest thing about my job is that I get to wear really great clothes. I am the centre of my look. I am aware that people are interested in me because of what I do.*

Do you approach menswear differently to womenswear? *For me, there is not any difference between designing for a woman and designing for a man in that I want to make them both look great. And so I have to find a way to do it. If I am developing a cutting technique, I will explore it in both the men's and women's clothes and, similarly, if I find an amazing yarn or fabric I will develop them in both the men's and women's line.*

Who are your design icons? *People say my fashion is avant-garde, but it is true that it uses the past as an inspiration. I go to museums and look at paintings, particularly eighteenth-century French art and painters such as François Boucher and Jean-Honoré Fragonard. The important thing is to understand the world in which you live, but you cannot do it from here, you have to look to the past.*

What are the pros and cons of working in London for a designer? *London is an amazing city. There's nowhere in the world like it – it's so large. You sense the whole history. England is a place of great tolerance compared to other countries – maybe not always, but that's what it evolved to be somehow. It's an amazing city.*

Does British fashion history ever inform your work? *I am English, so it is impossible for me to ignore British culture in my designs. The fabrics I use are often traditional British fabrics, for example, English flannel, which benefit from classic British manufacturing techniques, as represented by the Savile Row tradition.*

Is your logo British or global? *The Vivienne Westwood signature orb symbolizes the world, yet it is quintessentially British, part of the historical royal regalia held by the Queen during the ceremonial opening of Parliament. The logo stands for 'taking tradition into the future,' where the orb represents tradition and the past and the future is symbolized by Saturn's orbital ring.*

Do you think there is a distinct British style? *I think in the case of English men, they are more adventurous than women. I used to work in my shop, World's End, and if a man and a woman came in together and they were shopping for him, well, he'd choose something and she'd persuade him to put it back. On the other hand, he'd be pushing her in some direction she hadn't been before. In general, men are more adventurous in England.*

Which other British designers do you admire and why? *There are some good designers around at the moment, doing very, very nice things. I guess some designers are constantly going through the magazines looking at what's going on to have a sense of what is contemporary and wanted, you know, the kind of thing that people would like to have, what is actual and what is current.*

Are you ever completely satisfied or are you a perfectionist? *I am never completely satisfied* ⬛⬛

| **p.202** | bottom left Bouquets of flowers artwork; bottom right Lace pattern | **p.203** | Sequined jumpsuit from the 'Innocent' collection, A/W 2006

Aitor Throup
| **opener** | Jez Tozer; styling Stephen Mann; animation Daniel Gill & Anna Sheldon
| **p.15** | All Jez Tozer | **p.16** | Jez Tozer | **p.17** | Top left & right courtesy of
Topshop; all other images courtesy of Aitor Throup | **p.18** | Bottom left Jez Tozer;
all other photography courtesy of Fourmarketing for Stone Island | **p.19** | Bottom
left & right courtesy of Fourmarketing for Stone Island | **p.20** | All Jez Tozer

Alexander McQueen
| **opener** | John-Paul Pietrus www.johnpaulpietrus.com, styling by Loïc Masi,
hair by Laurent Philippon at Calliste, make-up by Christelle Cocquet at Calliste,
model Vala at 2PM | **p.29** | Middle www.catwalking.com
All other photography courtesy of Alexander McQueen

Boudicca
| **opener** | Justin Smith | **p.32** | All imagery courtesy of Boudicca | **p.33** | Top
left Miguel Villalobos www.miguelatmiguelvillalobos.com; bottom left Huw Morgan
| **p.34** | All imagery Boudicca | **p.35** | Justin Smith | **p.36** | Top left model Keira
Gormley at Storm Models; top right Bumble & Bumble; all bottom Miguel Villalobos
www.miguelatmiguelvillalobos.com | **p.37** | model Wei Chiung Lin at Union Models

Burberry Prorsum
| **opener** | Will Davidson M.A.P, styling by Karen Langley & Katie Shillingford,
hair by Teddy Charles, make-up by Romy Soleimani, retouching by Morph Retouch
All other photography courtesy of Burberry

Cassette Playa
| **p.49** | Top left & right Anne De Vries & Melanie Bonajo, model Finbar; bottom
left & right Anne De Vries & Melanie Bonajo, model Carl | **p.50** | Bottom left
model Saskilla | **p.52** | Top left & right Takashi Kamei, models Leke & Decio;
bottom Simian Coates, models Dave & Adam

Christopher Kane
| **opener** | Matt Irwin | **p.56** | All Claire Robertson | **p.58** | Top left Claire
Robertson | **p.59** | Jason Evans | **p.61** | Middle & bottom left Claire Robertson
All other photography courtesy of Christopher Kane

Danielle Scutt
All photography courtesy of Danielle Scutt

Deryck Walker
| **opener** | Josh Olins | **p.68** | All Cleon Manz www.cleonmanz.com for
www.fashion156.com, creative direction by Guy Hipwell at www.fashion156.com,
make-up by Lan Nguyen, hair by Perry Patraszewski, styling assistance by Liz Dye,
Afra Blake & Gemma Roberts, model Tobias S at Premier | **p.69** | courtesy of Deryck
Walker | **p.70** | Top left, middle & right Wes Kingston; all other imagery courtesy
of Deryck Walker | **p.71** | Top right Jean Francois; bottom right courtesy of SWG3
gallery; all other imagery courtesy of Deryck Walker | **p.73** | Bottom Ben Charles
Edwards for www.fashion156.com, creative direction Guy Hipwell at Fashion156, model
James Meron at Models 1
All other imagery courtesy of Deryck Walker

Eley Kishimoto
| **opener** | Jake Walters | **p.77** | Top left, middle right, bottom left & right Kumi
Saito | **p.80** | Top left Stephanie Solinas, models Julian Dykmas and Lou Savoir; top
right Stephanie Solinas, models Chris Pfanner and Anja Reiner, both images courtesy
of Eastpak | **p.81** | Heather Favell, model Lauren Van Hooser at Next Models Miami
All other images courtesy of Eley Kishimoto

Emma Cook
| **opener** | Julia Kennedy, styling by Gemma Hayward | **p.86-87** | Top left & bottom
right Claire Robertson | **p.88-89** | Top right & bottom left Simian Coates
All other photography courtesy of Emma Cook

Gareth Pugh
| **opener** | Claire Robertson | **p.92-93** | Top & bottom right Matt Irwin | **p.94** |
Nagi Sakai, styling by Sasa Thomann, hair by Bok-Hee at Streeters, make-up by
Munemi Imai at See Management, model Barbara Garcia at Ford | **p.95** | Top right
Jason Evans; bottom Simian Coates | **p.96** | Top Jason Evans; middle right Claire
Robertson | **p.97** | Claire Robertson
All other photography courtesy of Gareth Pugh

Giles Deacon
| **opener** | Sølve Sundsbø / Art + Commerce | **p.100** | Courtesy of Giles Deacon
| **p.101** | Top right & middle left Claire Robertson; all other photography courtesy
of Giles Deacon | **p.102-103** | Top left Claire Robertson; right Simian Coates; left
middle, bottom & opposite page Patrick Lindblom www.patricklindblom.com | **p.104** |
Bottom right Claire Robertson; all other imagery courtesy of Giles Deacon
| **p.105** | Matt Irwin

Hussein Chalayan
| **opener** | Nick Knight / Vogue © The Condé Nast Publications Ltd | **p.108** | Top
left, middle right, bottom & middle left Claire Robertson | **p.112** | Photograph
www.catwalking.com
All other photography courtesy of Hussein Chalayan

John Galliano
| **opener** | John-Paul Pietrus, www.johnpaulpietrus.com, styling by Loïc Masi, hair
by Vinz at B Agency, make-up by Greshka, model Vala at 2PM
All other photography www.catwalking.com

Jonathan Saunders
| **opener** | Clive Booth www.clivebooth.co.uk | **p.124** | Jason Evans | **p.125** |
Top right Claire Robertson; top middle & left Jason Evans; bottom Clive Booth
www.clivebooth.co.uk | **p.126-127** | Top Clive Booth www.clivebooth.co.uk
All other photography courtesy of Jonathan Saunders

Julien Macdonald
| **p.130** | Bottom middle www.catwalking.com | **p.133** | Bottom MJ Kim/Getty
All other photography courtesy of Julien Macdonald

Louise Goldin
| **opener** | Darren Cresswell | **p.136** | Courtesy of Louise Goldin | **p.137** | All
Jason Lloyd-Evans | **p.138** | Top left, right & middle left Claire Robertson; bottom
Simian Coates | **p.139** | Simian Coates

Luella
| **opener** | Mark Pillai, styling by Jacob Kjeldgaard, model Kinga Rajzak
| **p.142-143** | Top www.catwalking.com | **p.144-145** | Bottom www.catwalking.com
All other imagery courtesy of Luella

Matthew Williamson
| **opener** | Matthew Shave www.matthewshave.com | **p.149** | Bottom Peter Zownir
www.zownirphotography.com | **p.150** | Middle right Matthew Shave www.matthewshave.com
All other photography courtesy of Matthew Williamson

Nathan Jenden
| **both openers** | John-Paul Pietrus, www.johnpaulpietrus.com, styling by
Joan Campbell, hair by Asashi at Caren, make-up by Liz Martins at Naked, model
Tao Okamoto at Premier | **p.154** | Top left & right Simian Coates | **p.155** | All
courtesy of Nathan Jenden | **p.157** | John Laurence, model Sarah Seewar at Storm
Model Management

Noki
| **opener** | Morgan White, styling by Kim Howells, hair by Aimee Robinson for Tommy
Guns using Bumble and Bumble, make-up by Mel Arter at CLM using MAC Cosmetics,
model Emma at IMG | **p.160-161** | All Morgan White, styling by Kim Howells
| **p.162-163** | All photography courtesy of Noki

Thank you to all the inspirational designers and their teams for being a part of the British Designers book. Thanks to the press agents for their patience and for supporting the idea. Many thanks to all those who generously gave imagery, time for interviews and allowed access to their design practice. A special thanks to Lee Widdows, Willie Walters and Louise Wilson – all at Central St Martins, the greatest art school in the world, without which this book would not exist. A special thanks to Nick Knight for writing the foreword and providing an amazing cover image, and to Charlotte Knight and the whole SHOWstudio team for their support. Thanks to all the photographers for providing fantastic images. Thank you to Penny Martin for her invaluable guidance and also to Harriet Quick and Mandi Lennard for their time. Thanks to everyone at Laurence King and the team that worked on the book: Helen Evans, Melissa Danny, Evi Peroulaki, Ida Riveros, Catherine Hooper and Lewis Gill. Finally a titanic recognition to byBOTH for brilliant art direction.

Aitor Throup *www.aitorthroup.com*
Alexander McQueen *www.alexandermcqueen.com*
Boudicca *www.platform13.com*
Burberry Prorsum *www.burberry.com*
Cassette Playa *www.cassetteplaya.com*
Christopher Kane *www.relative-london.com*
Danielle Scutt *www.daniellescutt.com*
Deryck Walker *www.deryckwalker.net*
Eley Kishimoto *www.eleykishimoto.com*
Emma Cook *www.emmacook.co.uk*
John Galliano *www.johngalliano.com*
Gareth Pugh *www.garethpugh.net*
Giles Deacon *www.relative-london.com*
Hussein Chalayan *www.husseinchalayan.com*
Jonathan Saunders *www.jonathan-saunders.com*
Julien Macdonald *www.julienmacdonald.com*
Louise Goldin *www.relative-london.com*
Luella *www.luella.com*
Matthew Williamson *www.matthewwilliamson.com*
Nathan Jenden *www.nathanjenden.com*
Noki *www.novamatic.com*
Paul Smith *www.paulsmith.co.uk*
Philip Treacy *www.philiptreacy.co.uk*
Preen *www.preen.eu*
Stella McCartney *www.stellamccartney.com*
Stephen Jones *www.stephenjonesmillinery.com*
Vivienne Westwood *www.viviennewestwood.com*